Brian Sears is a trained teacher with nearly 40 years' experience of primary education. He was head teacher at Yorke Mead School, Croxley Green, Hertfordshire from 1980 until his early retirement in 1997 and now continues teaching in one-to-one private tuition.

In 1984 Brian had six stories published by NCEC in an anthology, A Yearful of Stories, and has contributed to the SU Bible reading notes Snapshots, for primary school-aged children. For the last seven football seasons, Brian has realized his other passion, in that he has written a weekly column in the Independent based around statistics of Premiership football. Four years ago, Scripture Union and CPO jointly published Brian's record of Christians working in the football industry, Goal! Winning, Losing and Life, the writing of which involved Brian in meeting the likes of Cyrille Regis and in a memorable visit to Old Trafford to interview Manchester United's secretary and chaplain.

Brian frequently leads church services by invitation in Hertfordshire, mainly in the Baptist tradition. He is an enthusiastic Watford FC supporter, two highlights being the play-off victory four years ago at Wembley and telling a story about Timothy Bear at the club's annual Carol Service.

D1649477

Text copyright © Brian Sears 2006
Illustrations copyright © Mary Hall 2006
The author asserts the moral right
to be identified as the author of this work

Published by
The Bible Reading Fellowship
First Floor, Elsfield Hall
15–17 Elsfield Way, Oxford OX2 8FG
Website: www.brf.org.uk

ISBN 1 84101 394 3
ISBN-13 978 1 84101 394 7

First published 2006
10 9 8 7 6 5 4 3 2 1 0

Acknowledgments
Unless otherwise stated, scripture quotations are taken from the
Contemporary English Version of the Bible published by
HarperCollins Publishers, copyright © 1991, 1992, 1995
American Bible Society.

A catalogue record for this book is available from the British Library

Printed in Singapore by Craft Print International Ltd

Through the year with
Timothy Bear

—— 24 five-minute stories ——
for special days and seasons of the year

Brian Sears

Acknowledgments

It was the staff and children of Yorke Mead School, Croxley Green, who over the years encouraged my first attempts to tell these stories. In more recent times, it has been Cassiobury School, Watford (where I was a founder pupil in 1951), and Little Green School, Croxley Green (where I began my teaching career in 1967), that have supported me in getting them ready for publication. Mrs Chris Luddington, who has had connections with all three schools, has added her current professional expertise in many helpful suggestions. I am grateful also to my family and especially to my wife, Ros.

Preface

Below are some of the comments from children who have enjoyed the Timothy Bear stories.

I think you have great stories because sometimes they're funny and sometimes they're sad but I like them however they are.
ALICE

I really like the way you set the story out and the way you get the message out.
NATALIE

I enjoy hearing Mr Sears' stories always. They make me feel warm inside on a Tuesday morning whatever they're about.
GEORGE

The stories are cool! The Timothy Bear ones are the best even though I don't support Watford! Timothy rocks!
INDIA

Maybe you can make the stories into a play. Timothy is the best. You should also add some girls.
AMY

I like the funny parts of these stories. Next time make them longer so I'll be able to catch more. I'm always at my violin lesson.
RACHEL

I think these stories are brilliant and should be known worldwide. I hope he writes more.
MARCIA

Contents

Introduction 11

Autumn term

A story for the new school year 14
Timothy Bear and his glasses

A story for harvest 18
The special apple

An autumn day story..23
Watch it!

A story for Hallowe'en 27
The Hallowe'en angel

A story for Guy Fawkes day 31
Timothy Fawkes

A story for Remembrance 36
Poppies for remembrance

An Advent story 40
Timothy and the innkeeper's boy

A story for Christmas..44
Tim-in-the-box

Spring term

A snowy day story 51
The expert at making heads

A story for Epiphany 54
Timothy Bear and the Christmas card

A Shrove Tuesday story 60
A surprising pancake day

A story for Lent 64
The cup run

A story for Mothering Sunday 68
The double celebration

A Palm Sunday story 72
The day of the donkey

A Good Friday story 76
Prince Timothy and the sale

A story for Easter Sunday..81
The new Timothy Bear

Summer term

A story for Pentecost 88
Timothy Bear has a quiet time

A story for Trinity 92
The clock party

A story for Ascension day 96
In touch

A story for St George's day 101
Dragons

A story for early summer 105
The bluebell woods

A story for Father's day 109
A welcome load of rubbish

A story for the time of the school play 113
The good prop

A story for summer 117
The beach day

Index of PSHE links..121

Index of Bible links 123

Instructions for making a paper boat 124

Introduction

In this book you will find a wealth of five-minute stories for all major special days throughout the school and Christian year. Each term also includes a seasonal story, providing a progressive link for the teacher and an ongoing appeal for the child.

The 24 stories are all based on the character of Timothy Bear, who, together with his family and friends, finds himself at the centre of many adventures guaranteed to appeal to 5–7 year olds. Each story has been devised to help those working with young children to teach biblical and moral truths through the medium of story. Each story includes:

- A seasonal theme
- PSHE links
- Bible links, including the key passage in full
- Follow-up material for the assembly or classroom, including ways to help young children to:
    - get to grips with the story
    - express the story
    - own the story
    - live out the story

The stories can be used in collective worship and assemblies, PSHE and circle time, as an aid to the teaching of RE, or purely for enjoyment at story time.

Autumn term

A story for the new school year

Timothy Bear and his glasses

 PSHE link

Breadth of study 5b: Pupils should be taught to feel positive about themselves (for example, by having their achievements recognized and by being given positive feedback about themselves).

 Bible link

God gives helpful advice to everyone who obeys him and protects all those who live as they should.
PROVERBS 2:7

Timothy Bear is not very good at coping with changes, and a lot of changes were about to happen. Holiday time would change back to school time, and that would mean a new teacher.

'I liked Mrs Tudor so much,' Timothy said to Mrs Bear. 'Miss Read sounds much too strict.'

On top of everything else, Timothy was going to have to

wear glasses for the first time. No one else in his class wore glasses. Timothy would be the odd one out. Mrs Bear had read out part of the letter from the optician: 'Timothy will need to wear glasses all day long, at home and at school.' Not only was he going back to school with a new teacher, but he would look so different as well.

It was very strange going back to school on the first day of term. Timothy had to be careful. Up to then, he hadn't given much thought to lampposts, crossing the road, or other people. Today he was almost bumping into things and tripping over other things. He was glad when he reached his friend Claude's house, but a moment later Timothy Bear was furious.

'Hi, four-eyes!' Claude said, bursting out laughing.

Timothy whipped the glasses from round his head and stuffed them in his pocket. No one else was going to have the chance to make fun of him.

Back at home, Mrs Bear thought she ought to explain to Timothy's head teacher why he would be wearing glasses in school. Miss Bridge understood and promised over the phone to check that everything was all right.

Later that morning, Miss Bridge kept her promise. She soon picked out Timothy Bear *without* his glasses, and had a whispered conversation with Miss Read.

'Timothy, come with me, please,' said the head teacher. Timothy wasn't too eager but he had to go. In the head's room, it was a bit like being at the optician's again. Miss Bridge started playing a game. She pointed to the two numbers '2' and '5' in a long line of numbers and asked Timothy to add them together. Because of his poor eyesight, Timothy thought she was pointing to the '3' and '6'.

'That's easy,' he said. 'They make 9.'

Miss Bridge was now sure that Timothy's sight was letting him down, because she knew he was good at numbers.

'Empty your pockets!' said Miss Bridge sternly. The glasses tumbled out with all the other things.

'You must wear these, Timothy,' said Miss Bridge handing them to him. 'We must improve that eyesight of yours.'

No one laughed when Timothy, glasses and all, returned to the classroom. The teacher fixed the class with a steely 'laugh if you dare' type of look. By then, Miss Read had had one of those brainwaves that teachers wish would come even more often.

'We're going to do some acting this afternoon. It's about a school called Hogwarts. We will need a girl to play the part of Hermione.'

Several girls were keen, and Miss Read decided the part should go to Amanda.

'There's a boy called Ron.'

Miss Read chose Claude for that part.

'And then there's Harry Potter.'

Everyone volunteered to be Harry, even the girls. Claude wished he wasn't Ron.

Miss Read went on. 'I will draw a scar on Harry's forehead, but he'll need to be good at catching and wear glasses.'

Everyone looked at Timothy. Hands and paws went down. Timothy was the obvious choice to be Harry Potter. All the class wished they were wearing glasses, especially when Timothy caught the Snitch to win the Quidditch match.

That evening, Mrs Bear was keen to know how the day had gone.

'Great,' said Timothy.

'And what's Miss Read like?'

'Great,' said Timothy. 'She's especially good at giving the right parts in plays to the right person.'

Helping children get to grips with the story

★ What new things were making life hard for Timothy?
★ Did Claude help his friend?
★ Why was the idea that came to Miss Read a brainwave?

Ways for children to express the story

★ Draw Timothy Bear with his glasses on.
★ Do some number line sums.

Helping children to own the story

★ What are some new things that you like?
★ Can you remember anything unkind that has been said to you?
★ Can you remember unkind things that you have said to others?

Ways for children to live out the story

★ What are some of the best things that you enjoy about school or home or church?
★ Timothy wore his glasses and they made him feel different from everyone else. Has anything like that happened to you? What was it?

Carry on the sentence: When someone teases me I feel…

A story for harvest

The special apple

PSHE link

Knowledge, skills and understanding 2e: Pupils should be taught to realize that people and other living things have needs, and that they have responsibilities to meet them.

Bible link

Generosity will be rewarded.
PROVERBS 11:25

In Timothy's garden, there's just one apple tree. In a good year there are lots of apples on it, with bright red cheeks. This year, one special apple caught Timothy's eye. It was the largest and shiniest. It was growing right on the topmost branch. When Mr Bear picked the apples, he couldn't quite reach it so he left Timothy's special apple to get even bigger.

'It's my apple,' thought Timothy. 'It will be the juiciest I've ever eaten.'

Timothy sat for a long time under the tree, staring up at his apple. At last he could be patient no longer.

'It's time for that last apple to come down,' he told Mr Bear.

For once, Mr Bear agreed. 'I'll climb up and get it,' he said.

Although Mr Bear could climb well, he was just unable to reach the special apple.

'I'll have to shake the branch and make it fall off,' he called to Timothy.

'Don't worry, I'll catch it,' shouted back the confident Timothy.

Mr Bear shook the branch and, sure enough, the apple began its fall through the branches. Timothy swayed this way and that, following its course until the apple landed safely in his outstretched paws. It was a very good catch and it was indeed a very good apple. It was even larger and even rosier now that Timothy could inspect it closely.

'That's a special apple,' said Mr Bear, puffing a bit as he jumped down next to Timothy. 'We must take it to church on Sunday for the harvest festival.'

'Hey, it's my special…' began Timothy, but Mr Bear had already turned away to rub the apple on his duster. Timothy knew it would be pointless to argue once Mr Bear had made up his mind.

On Sunday, Timothy could see his special apple from where he was sitting in church. It shone so brightly and looked so large. It was in front of a large marrow, and between a bunch of grapes and some sticks of celery. Timothy still wondered why it had to be given away. It would have made a lovely feast and, after all, he had watched it and caught it.

Mr Fairfield was leading the service. He always did at harvest, as he was a local farmer and knew about growing things. After they finished singing 'All things bright and beautiful', Mr Fairfield began his talk.

'I'm looking for something bright and beautiful,' he started, looking over the harvest display. 'Just the thing!' he said triumphantly, and he went straight to Timothy's apple.

'This is a very special apple,' he said, holding it up for everyone to see. 'It needed a lot of sunshine to make it as bright and red as this,' he continued thoughtfully. 'I wonder who sent the sunshine…'

'God did,' said a girl in a blue dress.

Mr Fairfield nodded. 'I wonder who sent the rain to make it so juicy…'

'God,' called Teresa, Timothy's sister.

'And who gave us trees and fruit to enjoy?'

Lots of hands went up this time.

'God,' said a boy with fair hair.

'Well done, all of you,' said Mr Fairfield, pleased with the way his talk was going.

'One last question. Who would you say this apple really belongs to?'

Timothy wanted to put up his paw and say 'Me!' but everyone answered, 'God!'

Mr Fairfield looked all round the congregation until he saw Mrs Furr. Mrs Furr was an elderly lady who was pushed to church in a wheelchair, as she found it so difficult to walk.

'I know that Mrs Furr loves apples,' said Mr Fairfield, 'but when she had to move to her flat she had to give up her garden and her apple trees. We're going to give this apple to her. Who'd like to take it to her?'

Hands and paws stretched to be chosen. Somehow Mr Fairfield spotted Timothy.

'Yes, that young bear there. You be our delivery boy.'

Timothy moved forward. He took the special apple from Mr Fairfield. He walked carefully to where Mrs Furr was sitting in her chair. Timothy placed the apple in her bony hands.

'Oh, it really is God's special apple,' murmured Mrs Furr.

'Yes, I know,' said Timothy, and the smile on the old lady's face was matched by the smile on his own.

Helping children get to grips with the story

★ Why did Timothy think the apple belonged to him?
★ Why did Mr Fairfield think that God had more to do with the apple?
★ Why was it a good idea to give the apple to Mrs Furr?

Ways for children to express the story

★ Draw a picture of the apple falling.
★ Draw Mrs Furr's face and Timothy's face.

Helping children to own the story

★ What things do you especially enjoy about harvest?
★ What ways are there for us to be selfish?

Ways for children to live out the story

★ Why do you think lots of schools and churches have harvest festivals and bring flowers, fruit, vegetables and other items of food to them? What is done or could be done with the gifts afterwards?

★ Is there someone you can help by giving them something or some time, or by cheering them up?

★ Can you think of something you could share with someone else that would make them very happy? For example: I could share some time with Grandma because she gets lonely now she's on her own.

★ Does it really matter if we share things?

Carry on the sentence 'I think we should share our things because…' or 'I don't think we should share our things because…'

An autumn day story

Watch it!

 PSHE link

Skills, knowledge and understanding 4d: Pupils should be taught that family and friends should care for each other.

 Bible link

Do yourself a favour by having good sense—you will be glad you did.
PROVERBS 19:8

It was a Saturday morning in October when the tune of 'Teddy bear's picnic', coming from Teresa's bedroom, woke up Timothy Bear. It was only six o'clock! Then Timothy remembered that Mr and Mrs Bear had given Teresa a super new watch as a surprise present, and among all the other things it did was to play tunes as an alarm to wake you up. Mr Bear had set it for six o'clock.

'She'll be awake by then anyway,' he had said. 'You know how excited she'll be on the first morning.'

Teresa was still very excited at breakfast.

'Does anyone want to know the time?' she demanded.

'It's five minutes after the last time you told us,' smiled Mrs Bear. 'And remember, it's a special watch that you must only wear out-of-doors on special occasions.'

It was a beautiful autumnal morning, and all the family agreed when Mrs Bear suggested an outing to the woods across the park near their house. Teresa knew it was not a 'special' outing, but she must wear her new watch. What if she met up with some friends?

It was a lovely walk to get to the woods. The sunshine made the trees seem to blaze with colour. The fallen leaves made a carpet just right for dragging paws through.

The family's favourite spot was the huge horse-chestnut tree with the shiny conkers nestling among the leaves on the ground. Timothy shuffled through the leaves like an express train, and where the leaves were thickest Teresa showed off her cartwheels that she was learning at school.

Mrs Bear had remembered to bring a plastic carrier bag so that she and Mr Bear could help Timothy and Teresa collect some interesting bits and pieces to take home.

Just as they were reaching home, Teresa wondered what time it was. As she pulled back the sleeve of her jumper, she realized that her watch had gone. She burst into tears and blurted out what had happened. Mr Bear promised to retrace their steps.

It was a fruitless search, and when he returned with nothing to report, Teresa's earlier excitement turned to misery. Her state of despair was punishment enough as the hours dragged by.

Timothy wished he could help his sister, and when the

brainwave came to him he hoped it would work. He sought out Mr Bear.

'May we go to collect some conkers… after the football results, please?' Timothy added almost as an afterthought. Mr Bear smiled his agreement. It was good that Timothy was showing an interest in the world about him.

The sun was low in the sky when father and cub set out. Bearchester United and Bearsfield Town had both won their games so there was a lot to be pleased about. Teresa, however, was still glum.

When they reached the conker tree, Mr Bear noticed that Timothy was listening as hard as he was looking for conkers. Then they both heard it at the same time: 'Teddy bear's picnic'.

'If you go down to the woods today, you're sure of a big surprise,' sang Timothy to himself, following the sound and unearthing the precious watch from under a thick pile of leaves. Mr Bear proudly patted Timothy's back.

'Well,' said Timothy modestly, 'I knew there were two six o'clocks in each day, and I guessed Teresa wouldn't have yet discovered how to make the alarm work only in the mornings!'

Mr Bear smiled. Timothy was already working out that he hadn't got the most technically-minded sister in the world!

'Look what your clever brother has found,' said Mr Bear to Teresa when they'd hurried home. Teresa could scarcely believe what she was seeing. Her excited early morning face made its reappearance. She even hugged Timothy when she heard the full story… and he was pleased to let her.

'As you go on learning to tell the time,' Timothy pointed

out to his sister, 'remember that the same time turns up twice every day.'

Helping children get to grips with the story

★ What big mistake did Teresa make?
★ What was Timothy's brainwave and why did he need to collect conkers 'after the football results'?

Ways for children to express the story

★ Make a pattern or picture of autumn colours.
★ Draw some watches or clocks with times on that you know.

Helping children to own the story

★ Talk about something you have lost. It may still be lost, or it may have been found.
★ Teresa was very disappointed to lose her watch. Are there any ways you might suggest to help her cope with that disappointment?
★ Mr and Mrs Bear decided not to add to Teresa's punishment, even though they had told her only to wear the watch on special outings. What was her punishment? Were Mr and Mrs Bear right not to add to it?

Ways for children to live out the story

★ Think of disappointments that have happened to you. Were they partly your fault? How can you cope with disappointments?
★ Can you think of anyone you can cheer up by a brainwave?

A story for Hallowe'en

The Hallowe'en angel

 PSHE link

Skills, knowledge and understanding 4a: Pupils should be taught to recognize how their behaviour affects other people.

 Bible link

The lifestyle of good people is like sunlight at dawn that keeps getting brighter until broad daylight.
PROVERBS 4:18

There's a lot about Hallowe'en that Timothy Bear doesn't like. It gives him a touch of the shivers! It's all right if he's wearing a mask, but some of his friends wearing masks make him feel scared. He's not sure about ghosts or witches either. Anyway, when his friends asked him to go out 'trick or treating', Timothy hesitated and then made excuses.

'I'd rather not. I might watch a video.'

'No loot, then, Timothy,' said David. 'Most people give us treats.'

Another concern in the back of Timothy Bear's mind was

the possibility of upsetting people. If *he* found some of the masks frightening, what about old people living on their own? What about Mrs Centurion, their next-door neighbour?

Mrs Centurion was still on his mind when he got home from school. Even watching his television programmes did not block her out.

'Do you think Mrs Centurion might like some company this evening?' Timothy asked Mrs Bear. 'We could play a game of chess.' Timothy was just getting the hang of chess, and Mrs Centurion had played it with her husband when he'd been alive.

'Let's phone up and see,' said Mrs Bear. She was pleased that Timothy was being so thoughtful, and realized why Timothy thought Mrs Centurion would value his company especially on Hallowe'en.

Mrs Centurion was delighted that Timothy could spare her some of his time.

'Take round a packet of these fruit lollies I've got in for any trick-or-treaters who might call,' said Mrs Bear.

Timothy and Mrs Centurion were engrossed in a game of chess when the bell rang for the first time. Mrs Centurion went to the door, wondering who could be calling so late. She stepped back when three masked figures were on her doorstep. Timothy was by her side.

'David, Michael and Lauren, isn't it?' he said cheerfully, recognizing his classmates.

'Trick or treat?' they said.

Timothy handed round the bag of lollies. Mrs Centurion had had time to realize what was happening. She closed her door.

'What a blessing you're here, Timothy. I remember being quite frightened on my own last year.'

Over the next hour or so, there was a procession of Hallowe'en visitors to Mrs Centurion's doorstep. Timothy and Mrs Centurion developed a pleasant line of conversation with the trick-or-treaters. They were a bit sorry that their chess was so often interrupted, though.

There was a longer gap until the final ring on the bell. Timothy couldn't recognize the pair of girls who were at the door in their witches' costumes. Timothy passed round the rapidly emptying bag of lollies.

'This is my Hallowe'en angel,' said a smiling Mrs Centurion, pointing at Timothy.

'But Hallowe'en is about witches and wizards,' blurted out one of the girls from behind her mask.

'I always mean exactly what I say,' said Mrs Centurion, giving Timothy a big wink.

Helping children get to grips with the story

★ Why didn't Timothy Bear go trick or treating?
★ What did he do instead?

Ways for children to express the story

★ Write down what you like or dislike about Hallowe'en.
★ Draw a picture of Timothy Bear as an angel.
★ If you were an elderly person living on your own, write down some of the things you might be thinking when your door bell rings after dark on Hallowe'en.

Helping children to own the story

★ What different things could you do on Hallowe'en?
★ Do you know any elderly people who might be lonely?
★ How might you help them?

Ways for children to live out the story

★ Do you agree with Timothy Bear and his feelings about Hallowe'en?
★ What can we do to help elderly people who live on their own all through the year and not just at Hallowe'en?
★ If people refuse to give treats, would it be right or wrong to play tricks on them?

A story for Guy Fawkes day

Timothy Fawkes

 PSHE link

Skills, knowledge and understanding 2c: Pupils should be taught to recognize choices they can make, and recognize the difference between right and wrong.

 Bible link

God sees that justice is done, and he watches over everyone who is faithful to him.

PROVERBS 2:8

Timothy Bear's school had celebrated Guy Fawkes night for quite a few years. It was much safer to have one big celebration on the school field than lots of smaller ones in back gardens. The PTA bought the fireworks and the dads were trained to set them off safely.

For weeks before the event, a bonfire grew in the corner of the school field. It grew because families in the community were clearing their gardens and were pleased to have somewhere to deposit what they no longer required, for burning.

Everyone reckoned this year's bonfire was the biggest and grandest ever.

When the great day arrived, Miss Bridge, the head teacher, said that the fire would be lit at seven o'clock. 'Entries for the Guy competition must be here by six-thirty,' she added.

Timothy Bear wanted to make a Guy, but it would have to be a last-minute job.

'On your way home from school,' Mrs Bear had said, 'go to the corner shop and get some sweets for the bonfire party.'

The corner shop was decked out for fireworks night. Timothy noted the chocolate bars with a free Guy Fawkes mask if you bought two. They would be part of his purchases. As he was working out the other items to buy, he overheard snatches of conversation between a boy and a girl a little older than himself.

'The size of that bonfire!'

'Let's set it going before anyone gets there!'

'Matches from home.'

'Great plan.'

Timothy Bear couldn't believe what he was hearing. How could anyone be so nasty as to spoil the fun of hundreds of people? As swiftly as Timothy made his purchases, the two plotters were out of the shop before him.

There was not a moment to lose. The Guy Fawkes mask swinging from his paw was forming a plan in his mind, especially as he knew a short cut back to the corner of the school field where the bonfire had been built.

Breathlessly, Timothy made it to the school field. A couple of discarded doors provided an easy route for him to climb to the top of the bonfire. He fixed the mask to his face, the elastic holding it round his head. Timothy Bear sat on top of the huge heap of rubbish as still as he could: Timothy Guy Fawkes indeed.

He did not have long to wait. The two troublemakers came the long way across the field, furtively glancing over their shoulders.

'We'll get the fire going and then escape through that path there,' whispered the boy, pointing at Timothy's short cut.

When they began striking the matches, 'Guy' went into action.

'Guy Fawkes for ever!' growled the masked Timothy and rolled over and over, with the doors acting like a slide. The youngsters froze like statues as Guy Fawkes hurtled towards them. But then, any bravado they might have had deserted them, and they turned on their heels, scattering matches on the damp ground. They had no wish to face up to a real-life Guy Fawkes. They were already outside the field, putting as much distance as possible between themselves and the Timothy Fawkes.

Timothy Bear took his time to stand up. He was surprised to hear a voice.

'The face belongs to Guy Fawkes, but the shape of the body is Timothy Bear.'

It was Miss Bridge, with a stern look on her face.

'I just glanced up from my work and, through my window, I saw the rolling of Guy Fawkes. You shouldn't have taken matters into your own paws, and you certainly shouldn't have climbed to the top of the bonfire.'

Timothy Bear pulled off his mask, looking downcast.

'Let's see you home,' went on the head teacher. 'And by

the way, you've already won tonight's new Guy competition. It will be called the Live Guy competition.'

'Guy Fawkes for ever!' growled Timothy, and even dared to wink at his head teacher.

Helping children get to grips with the story

★ What were some reasons for the school to hold a firework party?
★ What were the wrong things that the two children got up to?
★ How did Timothy Bear stop the two children spoiling the party?

Ways for children to express the story

★ Draw the shop window ready for Guy Fawkes night.
★ Draw Timothy as the Guy on top of the pile of wood and rubbish.
★ Draw the firework display that happened later.

Helping children to own the story

★ What things are done to spoil the places where we live?
★ What brave things can you remember being done in your family life or church life or school life?
★ What outdoor celebrations have you enjoyed attending?

Ways for children to live out the story

★ Timothy Bear, being a teddy bear, could stop bullies in special ways. How can bullies be stopped usually? Can we do anything to help?
★ Would it have been fair for the pranksters to light the fire? Why? Can you think of things that are not fair?

★ Was Timothy Bear's plan to save the bonfire a good one? Could it have been dangerous? In what ways?

.•

A story for Remembrance

Poppies for remembrance

 PSHE link

Breadth of study 5e: Pupils should be taught to meet and talk with people.

 Bible link

Do all you can for everyone who deserves your help.
PROVERBS 3:27

....

They were selling poppies at school. 'Poppies for remembrance,' said Miss Bridge, the head teacher.

Miss Read was keen that the children in her class should know what the poppy selling was all about.

'It's to remember times when our country has been at war. It's to remember those who fought and those who suffered,' Miss Read told the class. 'Tomorrow Mr Clark will come in to speak to us about it.'

Michael, in Timothy's class, got excited when war was being discussed. He was still excited while going home from school. He had a ruler in his pocket and jabbed it into children's backs, pretending it was a gun.

'Bang! Bang!' he shouted.

Michael even dared to go up behind an elderly man shuffling along the pavement wearing a green bobble hat.

'Bang!' screamed the over-excited Michael and dashed across the road as the elderly man slumped down by the garden wall. Timothy Bear had seen what happened and dashed up to make sure the man was not badly hurt.

'You're kind,' said the elderly man. 'It's just that I can't stand sudden loud noises. I'll get along now.' He struggled back to his feet and steadied himself with his sturdy walking-stick.

Timothy let him go, keeping an eye on him until he turned into a garden further along the street. Really, Michael would have to be more careful.

The next afternoon, Miss Read calmed her class to be ready for their visitor, Mr Clark. Timothy and David were sent to meet him in the entrance hall and escort him to their classroom. The only person in the entrance hall was an elderly man wearing a green bobble hat.

'Mr Clark?' asked Timothy.

'Why, it's my champion who saw me back on my feet yesterday!'

Back in the classroom, Miss Read introduced Mr Clark to everyone.

'Mr Clark was in our army during World War II,' said Miss Read. 'His memory is still very good even if his body gets a bit less nimble. Mr Clark will tell us what he remembers, and that will help us to remember.'

Everyone listened very hard as Mr Clark unfolded his story. He had been a soldier in France, and the army had been made to retreat. Shells and bullets made life very uncomfortable. In the end, a large splinter had entered his leg when a shell exploded near his tent.

'I've limped ever since, and I find loud bangs so hard to cope with.'

Timothy couldn't help glancing across at Michael, who was hiding his red face behind his hands.

Mr Clark had arrived home on one of the boats that made it into Ramsgate from Dunkirk. His leg had recovered a little in hospital.

'Don't ever think war is glamorous,' warned Mr Clark. 'And always think twice before playing with guns and pretending to shoot.' Again Timothy wondered how Michael was feeling.

Now Mr Clark helped to make poppies that were sold year by year so that the money raised could help those, like himself, who still suffered.

'As well as my painful leg, I regularly have nightmares,' continued Mr Clark.

When Miss Read asked if there were any questions for Mr Clark, the class showed how interested they had been by the thoughtful questions they asked. They gave him a long and loud clap when the time came for school to end. Miss Read's last words were to remind her class about poppies.

'Remember what Miss Bridge said about poppies for remembrance. You may buy them from the office on the way into school tomorrow.'

Timothy Bear was in early next morning with his money for a poppy. But even so, there was one member of his class ahead of him. It was Michael.

Helping children get to grips with the story

★ What bad and good things did Michael do in the story?
★ What did Mr Clark tell the class about his life?

Ways for children to express the story

★ Draw the elderly man with his walking-stick and green bobble hat.
★ Mr Clark said he still has nightmares. Write a list of the things that might be in the nightmares.

Helping children to own the story

★ What causes war?
★ What are some bad things that happen because of war?
★ Are there any good things that come from wars?

Ways for children to live out the story

★ Should we be careful about playing with toy guns?
★ In what other ways can we upset people?
★ Should we spare some of our money to buy poppies at Remembrance time? Why isn't each poppy given a price that we must pay?
★ What things can you do to avoid being 'at war' (arguing and fighting) with your friends?
★ What sort of things might become more difficult for you when you get elderly?

An Advent story

Timothy and the innkeeper's boy

 PSHE link

Skills, knowledge and understanding 1e: Pupils should be taught how to set simple goals.

 Bible link

Mary gave birth to her firstborn son. She dressed him in baby clothes and laid him on a bed of hay, because there was no room for them in the inn.

LUKE 2:7

Timothy Bear gets excited so early about Christmas that it makes him careless, and this year was certainly no exception.

'Your bedroom's a mess,' said Mrs Bear. 'Yesterday I tripped on a marble and had to put your toys away again.'

Timothy was forgetting his pleases and thank-yous as well.

At school, it was his paw-writing and his colouring that were going wrong.

'It's all so messy,' sighed Miss Read.

In fact, it was his carelessness that found Timothy in the school hall all on his own. He'd taken a photograph to show in assembly and had left it on the floor. Miss Read said he could go and get it.

Timothy was surprised at how dark it was in the hall, but then he remembered that the curtains were drawn so that they could start rehearsing this year's nativity play later that day. Already the stage blocks were out and a roll of corrugated paper was showing the walls of the stable. The door that swung on hinges had been much admired in assembly. Miss Read and the other teachers were good at this kind of thing.

Timothy had been a shepherd in last year's play. As he thought about it, somehow he felt drawn to the stable and sat for a moment on the stage block by the door.

Whether it was the darkness or the empty hall, Timothy didn't know, but suddenly he seemed to be floating through time and space. He was spinning but never dizzy, speeding but never frightened, and he landed with the slightest bump.

Timothy was still in a stable, but a real stable—a real stable with a real smell, and in the darkness he could make out the shape of a boy. The boy was wearing a short-sleeved robe and was working so hard. He was working around Timothy Bear —sweeping, putting things straight, tidying.

Timothy coughed nervously. The boy turned and smiled as if he expected to see him.

'Hello, Tubby!'

'Well!' thought Timothy, but he said, 'Good morning. Who are you?'

'My dad's the innkeeper and I'm doing some tidying up.'

'You're doing it very well. I'm not very tidy,' added Timothy.

'No, I'm not really,' went on the boy, 'but there's a feeling of something special in the air. I'm sure something special is going to happen, and I want to be ready.'

'Where are we?' Timothy wanted to know.

'This is Bethlehem,' said the boy. 'It's not an important place, but crowds of people are coming to fill in their census forms. The stars seem so bright and this stable of ours seems so still, as if it's waiting for something to happen.'

Timothy nodded. He was beginning to understand, but the boy was speaking again.

'It's not like me, but I want to be ready. I want it to look nice, smell nice. I've blocked up some of the draughts and I've tried to mend the door. I'm really pleased.'

Timothy opened his mouth, but nothing came out. He wanted to say, 'Yes, you're right. Something special is about to happen.' But he only nodded. Again the boy was talking.

'I feel so much better. I haven't enjoyed tidying up before, but this is different.'

Again Timothy's words wouldn't come out. He wanted to say, 'You're getting ready for a very special baby. He'll make all the difference in the world.'

Instead the boy said, 'What's that noise?'

This time Timothy did speak. 'It sounds like a donkey.'

Timothy was feeling that strange sensation again of floating through time and space. He was spinning but never dizzy, speeding but never frightened, and he landed with the slightest bump. He was on the stage block in his school hall. He picked up the photograph and returned to his classroom.

The innkeeper's boy was on his mind. Yes, he would really get ready for Christmas as well this year. He'd get ready carefully and tidily. If the innkeeper's boy could do it, so could he.

Helping children get to grips with the story

★ In what ways did Timothy get careless before Christmas?
★ Why was the innkeeper's boy being more careful than usual?
★ What special thing was about to happen in Bethlehem?

Ways for children to express the story

★ Draw the stage in the school hall, ready for the play.
★ Draw Timothy Bear travelling through time and space.

Helping children to own the story

★ What do you think you could get better at?
★ What happens to you and your friends when you get over-excited?
★ Have you ever been in a play? What was it like?

Ways for children to live out the story

★ How can you make life in your home even better than it is?
★ How can you make Christmas even better than it usually is?
★ What is Christmas really about?
★ What would you do to get ready if Jesus was coming to your home, your school, your church, or your neighbourhood?

A story for Christmas

Tim-in-the-box

 PSHE link

Skills, knowledge and understanding 1d: Pupils should be taught to think about themselves, learn from their experiences and recognize what they are good at.

 Bible link

When the men went into the house and saw the child with Mary, his mother, they knelt down and worshipped him. They took out their gifts of gold, frankincense, and myrrh and gave them to him. MATTHEW 2:11

Timothy Bear was wondering which part he would be given in this year's nativity play. Two years ago he had been one of the children of Bethlehem. Last year he had been a shepherd, and this year he would very much like to be a king.

Miss Thorn, Timothy's group leader, announced what was going to happen.

'We'll be doing our play in church the Sunday before Christmas. The whole congregation will be there. Claude, I want you to be Joseph, and Mary, it's your turn to be Mary the mother of Jesus!'

Everyone enjoyed the thought of Mary being Mary.

'Timothy,' went on Miss Thorn, 'I wonder if you'll be one of the kings?'

The delight on the face of Timothy Bear was answer enough.

'Which king would you like to be?'

'The one who carried the gold, please,' Timothy answered promptly. He wasn't very good at saying 'frankincense', and 'myrrh' always sounded sad.

When he arrived home, he couldn't remember who were going to be the shepherds. He couldn't even remember the other kings! Mrs Bear was delighted for him.

'I'll make a gold cloak for you, and we'll make a crown with jewels on it,' she said.

Busy Mrs Bear found time to do just as she had promised. It was a splendid cloak. Timothy helped with the crown. 'What shall I carry?' asked Timothy as Mrs Bear curled the card round his head to make sure it would be the right size.

Mrs Bear thought for a moment.

'There's the tin that Grandma's chocolates came in for your birthday. It's empty now and we could cover it with gold paper. That would be just the job.'

'Why did the king bring gold as a present?' asked Timothy as he cut out coloured shapes to make jewels. Mrs Bear smiled at yet another question.

'I guess he wanted to give the best and most precious present he could.'

Timothy was thoughtful, sticking the jewels on to the

crown. Mrs Bear was not surprised that quite a long time went by before he spoke again.

'I would like to bring something for Jesus,' he said slowly.

'Well, there's room in Grandma's tin. You could put something of yours inside.'

Timothy bounced upstairs. He remembered a spare 20p in his jacket pocket, and there was that tractor that had lost its wheel. They would fit in Grandma's tin. As he was coming downstairs again, he stopped. The king had given gold because it was the best thing he had. A spare 20p and a broken tractor did not match up to that. He went back to his bedroom to search again.

When Mrs Bear next saw Timothy, she could hardly see his face, as he was so loaded with presents to give. There was his favourite card game, a packet of biscuits that he kept for hunger emergencies, the 20p piece and a one-pound coin he'd saved up, his football annual and an almost-full box of chocolates.

'They'll never all go in Grandma's tin,' smiled Mrs Bear. Timothy had already thought of that.

'We could cover the box that all those envelopes came in, instead,' he said. Mr Bear had brought it home from work.

'That's a good idea, Timothy, but I still wonder if you're giving the best and most precious present of all.'

'What else is there?' asked a puzzled Timothy. It took Mrs Bear quite a while to explain what she meant.

The church was crowded on Christmas Sunday. In the hall at the back, the children were dressed and ready in good time. Then the play began.

Mary and Joseph looked really tired after their long

journey. The innkeeper shook his head sternly and then remembered the stable. The angels delivered their message to the shepherds very clearly. The shepherds hurried so much that one tripped up the step into the stable. And then it was time for the kings to make their way slowly down the centre of the church.

Many of the congregation smiled when they saw Timothy leading the way. His cloak was fit for a king and his crown shone—what could be seen of it, that is, because Timothy carried a huge cardboard box covered with gold paper. It was bigger than Timothy himself.

The kings reached Mary and Joseph and baby Jesus in the stable. They knelt and presented their gifts. Then everyone had a surprise. Instead of moving to the back with the other kings, Timothy sprang up high and landed right inside his gold-covered envelope box.

Miss Thorn put a hand to her mouth. Even she had not expected anything like this.

'You're like a Jack-in-the-box,' she whispered loudly.

'Not Jack. I'm Tim-in-the-box,' whispered back Timothy.

Pastor Hughes stepped forward with an even bigger grin than usual.

'Thank you all for a really lovely play,' he said to all on the platform. 'I don't think I've ever seen an ending like that before. But Timothy has set us all an example. He has given the most precious gift of all to baby Jesus. What a Christmas it would be if we all did the same! Mind you,' went on the Pastor with eyes twinkling and his fingers trying to do up his jacket buttons, 'an envelope box wouldn't do for me. I'd need an oil drum!'

Helping children get to grips with the story

★ What part was Timothy given for the nativity play and why was he so pleased?
★ What different things did Timothy think about putting in his box as gifts for the baby Jesus?
★ What did he finally put in the box?

Ways for children to express the story

★ Can you find the story about the kings? It's in the New Testament part of the Bible, in Matthew 2:1–12.
★ By talking with a friend, see how much of the story of the birth of Jesus you can remember between you.

Helping children to own the story

★ Make a list of the people in the nativity play. Which part would you like to play?
★ What things would you like to give to baby Jesus or any baby?

Ways for children to live out the story

★ Why was Timothy putting himself in the envelope box as 'the most precious gift of all'?
★ What sort of things can we do at home, at church, or at school to show that we are really part of them?
★ What would be the best thing about you that you could give?

Carry on the sentence: 'The best bit of me I could give would be to…' Examples: 'to play with my little brother or sister' or 'to listen to my friends when they're feeling sad'.

Spring term

A snowy day story

The expert at making heads

 PSHE link

Breadth of study 5h: Pupils should be taught to ask for help.

 Bible link

As soon as God speaks, the earth obeys. He covers the ground with snow like a blanket of wool.

PSALM 147:15–16

Timothy Bear wished it would snow. He wanted snow that would settle and last. Somehow his wishes didn't seem strong enough. When it was cold it rarely snowed, and even then the snow quickly melted away.

Timothy blamed it on Mrs Bear. She must have wishes that were very strong. 'I only hope it doesn't snow,' said Mrs Bear. 'It's the last thing we need!'

One day, at school, it was very cold outside and the class was having story time inside. Timothy decided he would do his strongest wish. He crossed his paws, shut his mouth tight and opened his eyes wide, wishing for snow. He listened hard to Miss Read's story at the same time.

Miss Read had an endless store of good stories and Timothy could see the pictures of the story in his mind's eye. When he glanced up at the window behind Miss Read, Timothy almost gasped out loud. It was snowing! Not thin, sleety snow but great lumps of it—snow that certainly intended to stay.

Timothy smiled to himself and listened to the rest of the story. He kept his paws crossed just to make sure.

When it was time to go home, a layer of snow was covering the gardens, the pavements and even parts of the roads. It was the turn of Penny's mother to see Timothy home. Mrs Bear was waiting at the gate, tight-lipped and miserable.

'What weather!' moaned Mrs Bear to Penny's mum.

'What weather!' thought Timothy to himself in quite a different kind of voice.

'Grandma's going to stay the night. She can't go home in this.'

Life couldn't be better, thought Timothy. Snow and Grandma both staying!

As Mrs Bear started making tea, Grandma dressed in her outdoor clothes.

'You're not going, Grandma?' asked Timothy.

'No,' answered Grandma, glancing at Mrs Bear. 'I'm taking my grandcub out in the garden to build a snowbear. Get your warm clothes on, Timothy.'

That's what Timothy liked about Grandma—she was always full of lovely surprises.

'Ridiculous,' said Mrs Bear. 'You two are as bad as each other.'

The snow was just right for building, and the snowbear grew quickly. It was going to be as tall as Timothy. Timothy and Grandma rolled a large snowball for the head, but when they put it in place it didn't look right at all. When they tried to improve it, they only seemed to make it worse.

'Your mum was the expert at heads when she was your age,' said Grandma at last. 'I wonder if she'd give us some help now.'

'I'll ask her,' said Timothy, sliding through the snow to the kitchen door.

'We need help with the snowbear's head,' blurted out Timothy to Mrs Bear, who had her hands in a bowl of flour. 'Grandma says you're the expert.'

'What nonsense!' said Mrs Bear. 'Make a snowbear at my age? What about tea? Do you want us all to starve?'

Then she stopped. In her mind's eye she was seeing herself as a young bear in her bobble hat as everyone admired her snowbear with its life-like head. She reached for her red scarf and red bobble hat.

'Well, I suppose if you really can't manage it, I can spare five minutes.'

When Mr Bear came home from work, he declared the snowbear to be the best he'd ever seen, especially with the red scarf and bobble hat round its splendid head. Timothy sat in the warm glow of the fire with the curtains drawn back. Hot tea, potatoes in their jackets and Grandma here to stay!

When it was bedtime, he went over to the window. It was still snowing and the snowbear stood firmly in the garden as if he was staying for at least a week.

'What weather, what super weather,' murmured Timothy Bear, and behind him Mrs Bear winked at the snowbear.

Helping children get to grips with the story

★ Say 'What weather' in the different ways used in the story and in other ways you might be able to think of.
★ What was the big problem that Timothy and Grandma found in making their snowbear?
★ What was the answer to their problem?

Ways for children to express the story

★ Draw a picture of Timothy's snowbear. You may need to find some dark paper and white crayons, chalk or pencils.

Helping children to own the story

★ What kind of weather do you like?
★ What things do you like to do if it snows?
★ Who would you like to come and stay at your house?
★ What lessons did Mrs Bear learn in the story?

Ways for children to live out the story

★ What things are each member of your family, group and class really good at? Have you told them about it?
★ Who are the people that help you to do things? How do they help you? Maybe different people help you in different ways. How might you thank them?

A story for Epiphany

Timothy Bear and the Christmas card

 PSHE link (with cross reference to English: En1: 3d)

Skills, knowledge and understanding 2b: Pupils should be taught to take part in a simple debate about topical issues and extend their ideas in the light of discussion.

 Bible link

When Jesus was born in the village of Bethlehem in Judea, Herod was king. During this time some wise men from the east came to Jerusalem and said, 'Where is the child born to be king of the Jews? We saw his star in the east and have come to worship him.' … Herod… asked them when they had first seen the star. He told them, 'Go to Bethlehem and search carefully for the child…' The wise men listened to what the king said and then left. And the star they had seen in the east went on ahead of them until it stopped over the place where the child was. They were thrilled and excited to see the star.

MATTHEW 2:1–2 AND 7–10

Mrs Bear had said it was almost time to take down the Christmas cards. Timothy felt sad about that. He liked Christmas!

Auntie Gladys was still staying, so Christmas couldn't be quite all over yet. She was dozing in her chair and Timothy was trying to draw some pictures to go in with the family's thank you letters. Teresa Bear was having a temper tantrum and had stormed upstairs. Sisters! Mr and Mrs Bear were back to being just as busy about the house as they had been before Christmas came.

One card in the row hanging above the television set caught Timothy's eye. It was a picture of kings riding through hill country on camels. A star shone in the sky ahead. One camel, smaller than the rest, had no rider—only bags containing luggage at her sides.

Timothy stared at the picture, wondering hard. He could almost hear the camel bells. He must have wondered very hard indeed, because suddenly he seemed to be floating through time and space. He was spinning but never dizzy, speeding but never frightened.

He landed with the slightest bump, swaying from side to side—and he really could hear the camel bells!

Timothy was holding on to a hairy neck, the neck of the smallest camel on the card, and they were moving. The kings wrapped their bright robes around them as the sky darkened towards night. A fresh breeze ruffled Timothy Bear's fur.

55

'Nice of you to drop on,' said a voice. 'What's your name?'

'Timothy, thank you. What's yours?'

'Clara,' said the camel, 'and it's nearly my bedtime.'

'They look very important,' said Timothy, pointing to the kings.

'Well, they are,' replied Clara. 'They boss me about. Many's the whipping I've had from them. They've got a lot on their minds—kingdoms to run, budgets to work out, reputations to look after.

'But they seem to be changing. They suddenly decided to leave their kingdoms behind them. They've never torn themselves away before. Things are looking up; they've been looking up—looking up to that star.

'Perhaps that's the difference. They've always looked down before, to count money or eat their feasts, or check their lists. But since they've started to see the star, it's much easier to get on with them. Why, they're almost human. The other day they even lightened my loads.'

'Hey! That's sudden!' cried Timothy Bear.

Clara had skidded to a halt along with the others, and Timothy grabbed pawfuls of hair.

'Are we there? It's only an ordinary house.'

Timothy stayed where he was as the kings dismounted. One king went to the door and turned to the others, nodding and smiling.

'I haven't seen him smile like that in all my life,' whispered Clara.

The kings went inside. Timothy could hear happy chatter and, from time to time, a baby gurgling. Then the first king came out and made straight for Clara. He led her right inside the house! Timothy clung on, stroking her neck.

'The baby camel and the baby boy,' announced a voice.

'And the baby bear,' thought Timothy.

The kings undid the bags at Clara's side and out came presents—strange, expensive presents. Timothy wished he had a ball or a car that he could give. The kings were bowing and Clara again whispered her surprise in Timothy's ear.

'All the time people bow to them. He's a very special baby. He's making all the difference to them and to me.'

'And to me,' whispered back Timothy.

That was the last he said to Clara. Again he was floating through time and space. He was spinning but never dizzy, speeding but never frightened. With the slightest bump he was back with his drawings and the card was in its place above the television. Mrs Bear rushed in to check the time.

'Look at this card,' said Timothy. 'It's special.'

'Me! Look at a card, with cakes in the oven. It's not still Christmas, you know!'

Auntie Gladys stirred in her chair.

'Please, Auntie, look over here.'

'Yes, my dear... but... I'm so sleepy...' and Auntie Gladys nodded off to sleep again.

Mr Bear came in to look in the sideboard.

'Please look at this card with me.'

'Sorry, not now. The bulb needs replacing in the cupboard under the stairs.'

Teresa was Timothy's last hope, but when he called upstairs she told him in no uncertain terms that she was getting her doll dressed for a party. Timothy sighed. His family were just as bad as those kings before they looked up. Perhaps they would look up soon. He had, and he would never forget it.

Something fell from his paw on to the carpet. He smiled as he picked it up. It was a tuft of camel's hair.

Helping children get to grips with the story

★ What was it about the Christmas card that particularly caught Timothy's attention?
★ How had the kings behaved before they started the journey?
★ What showed that they had changed?
★ In the end, what did Timothy hope would happen to each member of his family?

Ways for children to express the story

★ Find a favourite Christmas card or two. What do you like about them?
★ With a friend, talk about as much of the story of the three kings and the first Christmas as you can remember.

Helping children to own the story

★ How can the birth of Jesus make a difference to us?
★ The kings changed their way of seeing things. They 'looked up' instead of 'looking down'. In what ways can we 'look up'?
★ Teresa doesn't do very well in this story. How did she let herself down? Are we ever like her?

Ways for children to live out the story

★ How could you make more time to stop and think about making worthwhile differences?

★ Are there any ways that we can make a baby we know feel welcome?

A Shrove Tuesday story

A surprising pancake day

 PSHE link

Skills, knowledge and understanding 4b: Pupils should be taught to listen to other people and play and work cooperatively.

 Bible link

You are good to everyone, and you take care of all your creation.
PSALM 145:9

Mrs Bear started making pancakes as soon as Timothy and Teresa came home from school. They were keen to help mix up the batter. It was great blending in the flour, eggs and milk. Mrs Bear put oil in the frying pan and, when that was hot enough, in went the first helping of batter.

'I love that sizzling sound,' said Teresa.

'What a wonderful smell,' added Timothy.

Mrs Bear could judge just the right moment when a pancake was crisp enough underneath to be tossed. She flicked it up in the air and caught it so tidily back in the pan. Timothy and Teresa watched enthralled, and took it in turns to eat.

There were four things that they could add to their pancake: a squeeze of lemon, sugar, syrup and sultanas. But Mrs Bear's rule was no more than two additions to each pancake.

Mrs Bear was cooking the seventh pancake when the phone rang. 'That could be Auntie Joan about the wedding,' said Mrs Bear. 'I'll leave you in charge, Timothy.'

Teresa had gone into the lounge to eat her second pancake while watching television. Timothy took over. He could just make out from the conversation in the hall that it was indeed Auntie Joan, and the subject was clothes for the wedding. It would be quite a long call!

When Timothy gently shook the frying pan, he knew that the pancake was ready to be tossed, because it slid. Dare he follow his mum's example? Why not? He firmly held the pan's handle and flicked upwards. As it turned out, it was much too strong a flick and the pancake reached the ceiling, sticky side up.

'Oh no!' Timothy's paw covered his mouth and he sat down at the kitchen table. Mrs Bear bustled back into the kitchen. 'What on earth shall I wear?' she was saying. 'I haven't even got a hat.'

As Mrs Bear resumed her place at the empty frying pan, the missing pancake released its hold on the ceiling and fell down... right on to Mrs Bear's head. Both paws were now covering Timothy's mouth and he wondered what Mrs Bear was going to do.

To his great relief, Mrs Bear burst out laughing. 'But I don't think it will do as a hat for the wedding,' she said.

There was still batter left in the bowl when they'd had four pancakes each and couldn't possibly eat any more.

'I expect Mrs Centurion would like one,' said Timothy remembering the good appetite of their next-door neighbour.

'All right,' replied Mrs Bear. 'It will be a good size.'

A few minutes later, Timothy, with the pancake on a tray, and Teresa, with the fillings on another tray, were making their way next door. They had been so busy with the pancakes that they hadn't seen the fall of snow.

Mrs Centurion was pleasantly surprised to see her visitors and what they'd brought her. She'd forgotten all about pancake day.

'And while Teresa's keeping you company, I'll clear the snow away from the path to your gate,' offered Timothy, noticing a broom in Mrs Centurion's porch.

Timothy Bear thoroughly enjoyed himself piling up the snow. Teresa explained Mrs Bear's rule to Mrs Centurion about only two additions, and she chose sultanas and syrup.

'This is the best pancake day of my life,' she said, and Timothy and Teresa couldn't agree with her more.

Helping children get to grips with the story

★ How are pancakes made?
★ Why was Timothy left alone in charge in the kitchen?
★ What happened when Mrs Bear returned to the kitchen?
★ What were Mrs Centurion's surprises?

Ways for children to express the story

★ Draw Mrs Bear in her pancake hat.

Helping children to own the story

★ What are your favourite additions to have with pancakes?
★ Teddy bears are allowed to toss pancakes. What are the dangers of doing that?
★ When the pancake landed on Mrs Bear's head, Timothy wondered what she would do. What different things could she have done? What would you have done?

Ways for children to live out the story

★ How can we be helpful in the kitchen? What must we be careful about?
★ Is it only elderly people who need good neighbours? How can we be good neighbours where we live?

A story for Lent

The cup run

 PSHE link

Skills, knowledge and understanding 3a: Pupils should be taught to make simple choices that improve their health and well-being.

 Bible link

No one can live only on food. People need every word that God has spoken.

MATTHEW 4:4

When the football season had started, Timothy had joined Bearchester United. Bearchester United had lots of different football teams and Timothy started training with the youngest.

Timothy likes football and knows quite a bit about it. His liking for honey, however, means that he's a little overweight and not as mobile as others of his age. He's nowhere near as fast as his friend, David.

It was no surprise when David was selected as one of the wide strikers in the early games and Timothy's name was

64

nowhere to be seen, not even among the substitutes.

'Bad luck,' said David kindly, 'I thought you'd make it as a defender.'

'Don't worry,' replied Timothy. 'I'll still come to training and I'll be cheering you on in the matches.'

He was as good as his word. Bearchester United were having a good season. Timothy Bear supported them through thick and thin, in sunshine and in rain. Of course, he was so disappointed when his name never appeared on the team sheet.

Mr Taylor, the manager, explained that the team was only doing so well because of the various skills of the players and the good practice games they had. Timothy nodded and David slapped him on the back.

'You're part of that,' David whispered to Timothy.

The main cup competition started after Christmas, with the final always held on the Saturday before Easter Day. It would be great if Bearchester United had a good cup run. As they made progress through the early rounds, Timothy was caught up in the drama of it all. He really would like to be more involved. He even determined to give up eating honey for Lent! He'd get himself into better shape!

Mr Taylor referred to Timothy as the team's number one fan.

'I don't think you've missed a single game. Everyone in the team hears you cheering them on,' enthused the manager. Timothy not only cheered, he was learning all the time and often acted as the ballboy, fetching the ball back when it was kicked off the pitch.

The quarter-final was the most tense game of the season.

Bearchester United's opponents were their local rivals, and with ten minutes to go they scored the first goal. If it remained the only goal, Bearchester United's hopes of cup glory would be gone for another year.

Timothy's cheering had never been so urgent all season, and his enthusiasm took him up and down the touchline as Bearchester United mounted attack after attack. David was on top form, speeding trickily down the wing. The left back timed his tackle well and the ball flew off the pitch.

Timothy Bear was almost in just the right position. He flung himself to stop the ball and, in the same movement, returned the ball to David. David just as quickly threw in the ball to the overlapping back, who centred, and before their opponents' defences could do anything about it the tall central striker had headed the ball into the goal.

Moments later, the referee blew the final whistle and a replay had been secured. Bearchester United lived to fight another day.

'What an alert ballboy you are, Timothy,' said Mr Taylor smiling broadly. 'Well done.'

Others besides David were now slapping Timothy Bear on the back.

'And we're short of goalkeeper cover,' went on Mr Taylor. 'We'll have a look at you in training. With saves like that one on the touchline, I reckon you'll certainly make it as sub goalie on the bench.'

Timothy Bear beamed his pleasure. He would be quite satisfied with that.

Helping children get to grips with the story

★ What was the disappointment that Timothy had to put up with in regard to the football team?
★ In what ways did he show his support for his team?
★ What made Mr Taylor think Timothy might make a good goalkeeper?

Ways for children to express the story

★ Make up a game to practise catching balls of different sizes.
★ Draw a picture of Timothy making the crucial catch in the cup match.

Helping children to own the story

★ Lent is a time for being less selfish. How did Timothy Bear show that he wasn't being selfish? How can we be less selfish?
★ Timothy gave up eating honey. What could we give up that might help us and others?

Ways for children to live out the story

★ What disappointments have you known? How do you cope with them?
★ What would you like to be really good at? What can you do to begin to improve?

A story for Mothering Sunday

The double celebration

 PSHE link

Skills, knowledge and understanding 4d: Pupils should be taught that family and friends should care for each other.

 Bible link

You must love each other, just as I have loved you.
JOHN 13:34

One Sunday last year was a double red-letter day in the Bear household. It was special because Teresa's birthday fell on Mother's Day.

About a week before, Timothy and Mr Bear made their way up into the loft at the same time, leaving Mrs Bear downstairs to enjoy her favourite television programme. Both said each other's names at the same moment.

'Dad.'

'Timothy.'

'You bat first,' said Mr Bear.

'Well, I was thinking about Mum,' replied Timothy. 'She's

very good, isn't she? She's a smashing cook and all that. I thought I'd make her a present and card for Mother's Day like the ones they did on Blue Peter.'

'Good idea, Timothy,' said Mr Bear. 'Actually, I was thinking along the same lines about Teresa. She's a smashing cub.'

'She's not too bad, I suppose,' said her brother grudgingly.

'She's mad about her Barbie dolls,' went on Mr Bear, apparently not noticing Timothy's tone of voice, 'so I thought I'd make her a Barbie-sized dolls' house to keep them in.'

They congratulated each other on their good ideas and set about collecting the materials they would need.

They had not got very far with their plans and preparations when the signature tune of the television programme wafted faintly up the stairs, to be followed more strongly by Mrs Bear's voice.

'Timothy! It's your turn for washing up. I'm ready now.'

'Oh, blow!' said Timothy under his breath. Then, loud enough to reach downstairs, he continued, 'Can't Teresa help tonight? I'm very busy.'

'No,' came back Mrs Bear's voice . 'It's your turn. Anyway, what are you doing that's so important to keep you up there?'

'It's a secret,' shouted Timothy bad-temperedly.

'Really,' said Mr Bear, 'if you do appreciate Mum, surely you can help with the washing up. It's no good saying "thank you" one day a year with a card and a present, and being mean the rest of the time.'

Timothy understood what Mr Bear was saying. He made

his way down to the kitchen and the washing up.

He felt better when he climbed back into the loft. Mr Bear was sorting out his wood and screws. Timothy found a yoghurt pot and some tissue paper.

A few minutes later, Mrs Bear's voice again wafted upwards.

'Darling, will you tell Teresa her bedtime story tonight?'

'Oh dear,' said Mr Bear almost to himself. Then, raising his voice, he called, 'I'm just starting something. Can't you see to Teresa?'

'I've a pile of ironing that I must get done for tomorrow. Anyway, what are you up to?'

'It's a secret,' shouted Mr Bear bad-temperedly.

'Really,' said Timothy smiling, 'if you think you have such a smashing daughter, surely you can find time to tell her a story. It's no good…'

'All right!' interrupted Mr Bear. 'I know when I'm beaten. Both of us seem to have a lot of learning to do.'

He smiled at Timothy as he lowered himself down the steps. 'I'm going to tell your sister such a story. It will be about a monster with three green heads, five red eyes and no legs. And his name will be Timothy!'

Timothy returned Mr Bear's smile and made his best monster-like face.

Helping children get to grips with the story

★ What plans were Mr Bear and Timothy making?
★ What lesson did Timothy have to learn?
★ What lesson did Mr Bear have to learn?

Ways for children to express the story

★ Make a Mother's Day card of your own.
★ Draw a design of a home for toys that you have. You may be able to make a room from some kind of box: for example, a shoebox.

Helping children to own the story

★ In what ways can we say 'thank you' to people who look after us on ordinary days?
★ How can we show our love on special days like Mothering Sunday?

Ways for children to live out the story

★ It's often a good idea to make things for days like Mothering Sunday rather than to buy things. What sort of things could you make?

A Palm Sunday story

The day of the donkey

PSHE link

Skills, knowledge and understanding 2e: Pupils should be taught to realize that people and other living things have needs, and that they have responsibilities to meet them.

Bible link

When Jesus and his disciples came near Jerusalem, he went to Bethphage on the Mount of Olives and sent two of them on ahead. He told them, 'Go into the next village, where you will at once find a donkey and her colt.'

MATTHEW 21:1–2

Timothy Bear was in church on Palm Sunday. After the Bible reading about Jesus riding into Jerusalem on a donkey, the man at the front said, 'We will sing the song "Make way, make way".'

Timothy leaned forward for the hymn book, wondering about the first Palm Sunday. He must have wondered very hard indeed, for suddenly he seemed to be floating through time and space. He was spinning but never dizzy, speeding but never frightened.

The fantastic journey ended with the slightest bump. Timothy was sitting on a dusty track between small, flat-roofed houses. It was early in the morning. The rising sun cast long shadows.

Two donkeys—a mother and her young colt—were just waking. They were stretching to the end of the ropes that tethered them to a post. Timothy understood their conversation easily.

'But I want to give someone a ride,' the colt was saying.

'Be patient, Trotty,' answered his mother. 'You're nearly strong enough.'

Trotty wasn't convinced. 'You've been saying that for weeks now. Please let me give rides.'

Timothy Bear stepped out of the shadows and neither donkey seemed surprised to see him.

'I'm not very heavy. Could I have a ride, please?'

Trotty's mother smiled her agreement and Timothy, having untied Trotty's rope, climbed up five steps of the outdoor flight of stairs so that he was tall enough to reach Trotty's back.

What a ride it was! Up and down the village track, down to the well and across for a drink in the river. The sun was much higher in the sky when the wonderful journey was over. Timothy was delighted to be given a ride and Trotty was delighted to give it.

Trotty's mother enjoyed the peace and quiet as well. She watched Trotty stop by the steps so that Timothy could slide off his back. Then she heard the sound of footsteps that made her look round.

'King Jesus needs him,' one of the men was saying, 'he really does.'

The speaker took hold of Trotty's rope and nobody stopped him. Trotty's mother brayed as her rope too was untied. Timothy smiled at her encouragingly and followed the two donkeys down the dusty track that led out of the village towards the great city of Jerusalem.

The sun climbed until it was right overhead, and there was no shade to be found along the road when the crowd came. Excitement was in the air and Timothy Bear, mingling with the crowd, could see that Trotty was the centre of attention. A man was riding him, a man with kind hands and soft words, a man the crowd was hailing as a king. The street was being made soft with cloaks and palm leaves and Trotty was panting but happy.

Trotty's mother brayed with pleasure when she saw him. In a few moments, the procession had passed and all was quiet again. Timothy Bear made his way back to the village and found a little shade.

The shadows were long again when Trotty and his mum returned. Trotty was very weary but as contented as he had ever been. Timothy stroked him soothingly; then he found a pail of carrots and a bucket of water.

As Trotty fed eagerly and drank deeply, Timothy smoothed the donkey's back and then washed his dusty hooves. By now the people were returning as well.

'He's going to be a very special king,' one of them was saying.

'Yes,' said another. 'He's the king of love and peace.'

'I wonder what that means,' replied the first.

Timothy smiled. 'I know,' he thought to himself as he finished cleaning and grooming the last hoof of all.

Suddenly Timothy Bear was travelling through time and space—spinning but never dizzy, speeding but never frightened—until, with the slightest bump, he was back in church, still reaching for his hymn book and still in time to join in with 'Make way, make way'.

Helping children get to grips with the story

★ Why did Jesus specially choose Trotty to ride on into Jerusalem?
★ What were the worries that Trotty's mother had?
★ In what ways did Timothy help Trotty when Trotty came back home at the end of the day?

Ways for children to express the story

★ Find out as much as you can about donkeys. Draw pictures and make a list of up to ten things about them.
★ Draw a picture of the kind of house that was most common in the time of Jesus.

Helping children to own the story

★ Can you think why Jesus chose to ride on a very young donkey rather than a huge war horse?
★ Find the story of the first Palm Sunday in the Bible and share it together. You will find it in Matthew 21:1–11; Mark 11:1–11; Luke 19:28–38 and John 12:12–19.
★ How is Jesus different from a king or a queen in our world today?

Ways for children to live out the story

★ What are good ways of caring for animals?

A Good Friday story

Prince Timothy and the sale

✓ PSHE link

Skills, knowledge and understanding 1b: Pupils should be taught to share their opinions on things that matter to them and explain their views.

✓ Bible link

Jesus was taken away, and he carried his cross to a place known as 'The Skull'. In Aramaic this place is called 'Golgotha'. There Jesus was nailed to the cross.
JOHN 19:16–18

There was a bit of a fuss in the Bear family. There was going to be a charity sale and Mr and Mrs Bear wanted Timothy and Teresa to donate some of their possessions. Timothy wasn't so keen.

'You've got three or four Action Bears. Surely you can spare one of them,' said Mr Bear. 'And you had two football annuals for Christmas.'

Parents didn't understand. Timothy gritted his teeth. Plenty of others could help with the sale—Teresa, for one— but he could not spare anything.

He was still determined at bedtime. He was in no mood to say prayers, so instead he would play his pretend game that often ensured sleep came quickly. Should he be a detective? Should he be an international footballer? Or should he imagine what it was like to be a prince?

Yes, he'd be a prince. He saw in his mind's eye a room in a palace. It even contained a four-poster bed. There was a crown on his head. The wardrobes were full of clothes, the cupboards full of toys, and servants would come at the tug of a bell. He was Prince Timothy the First!

It was a lovely room, with a huge window that led to a balcony. Timothy went to look out, rather hoping that there would be crowds to see his crown and fine robes. But he looked out on a deserted courtyard—deserted except for one boy.

The boy was badly dressed in rags and he shivered in the cool breeze. Timothy felt his rich robe. He glanced at his wardrobes, bulging with every kind of clothing to dress up in or to wear for best. Should he send a cloak for the boy?

No, why should he? 'I'm a prince,' he said to himself. 'I'm Prince Timothy and I can do as I please.'

The boy below had a bowl in his hand. It was strange for a boy to carry a bowl. As Timothy watched, the boy put the bowl down in front of his feet.

It was a begging bowl—a begging bowl for food. It couldn't have been filled recently, for the boy looked so thin.

Timothy could just tug the bell and order a cooked breakfast, or chicken and chips, or trifle and ice cream. Should he send down a meal for the boy?

No, why should he? 'I'm a prince,' he said to himself. 'I'm Prince Timothy and I can do as I please.'

The boy in the courtyard felt inside his tattered pocket and pulled out a lump of chalk. He bent down and began to draw on the paving stones. Timothy could see the picture taking shape and admired the boy's talent. But a prince had so many exciting toys—cupboards full. Should he send down a toy for the boy?

No, why should he? 'I'm a prince,' he said to himself. 'I'm Prince Timothy and I can do as I please.'

It certainly was a well-drawn picture—of a hill outside a city, with three crosses on it. But just as the finishing touches were being added, it started to rain and the drops smudged the chalk picture.

The boy looked sad and the picture was soon washed away. He stood up, pocketed the chalk and, holding the bowl, began to walk away from the palace.

Timothy couldn't help watching as the boy made his way through the gate and into the distance. And suddenly he saw, as if for the first time, that the boy, too, was wearing a crown, but a crown of tangled thorns.

The boy turned once to look right up into the window. He had the kindest, strongest face Timothy had ever seen.

'Come back, come back!' called Timothy, but the boy had walked out of sight. 'Come back, come back!'

Mr Bear was shaking Timothy's shoulder. 'It's all right, I'm here.'

'Oh, I've been dreaming,' said Timothy. He could remember it all so clearly. 'I'll be all right now.'

He had made up his mind. He kept his dream a secret but he did go to the sale. He did give an Action Bear, a football annual and his whole collection of soldiers.

Mr and Mrs Bear were highly delighted. So was someone else as well: the boy in the dream.

Helping children get to grips with the story

★ What things did Timothy wonder about sending down to the boy in the courtyard?
★ What were the differences that the dream made to Timothy?

Ways for children to express the story

★ Draw your own picture of the one the boy drew in the courtyard.
★ Draw a picture of the boy walking away from Timothy.
★ Look in the mirror and show the face of Timothy when he was (a) watching the boy draw, (b) deciding not to give, and (c) wanting him to come back.

Helping children to own the story

★ What was making it hard for Timothy to get to sleep? Are there times when you find it difficult to get to sleep? Share with your friend things that help you.
★ Who do you think that Timothy thought the boy in the dream was? Can you give some reasons for your answer?

Ways for children to live out the story

★ What possessions would you be willing to give away for others to buy?
★ In what ways was Timothy Bear poor?
★ In what ways was the boy in the dream rich?
★ What can we learn about the ways we are poor or rich?

A story for Easter Sunday

The new Timothy Bear

 PSHE link

Skills, knowledge and understanding 2c: Pupils should be taught to recognize choices they can make, and recognize the difference between right and wrong.

 Bible link

On Sunday morning while it was still dark, Mary Magdalene went to the tomb and saw that the stone had been rolled away from the entrance.

JOHN 20:1

Grandpa Bear is a splendid character. He is known as Granbee to his friends and grandcubs, including Timothy. His family loves him so much, and they all think he's the best grandpa in the world. He has eyes of steel blue and a hearty laugh that makes you chuckle just to hear it.

Timothy longs to please him and hates to cross him, and, although Granbee often does unusual and surprising things, you always end up feeling better for being with him.

Take, for instance, Granbee's boat.

It was a sailing boat, smooth and beautiful to hold. Granbee had made it for Timothy and given it to him in time for the Easter holidays. The white sails even had the initials T.B. inscribed on them, to leave Timothy in no doubt that it was his.

'Never let go of this,' said Granbee as he handed over a ball of string that was fastened to the stern. Granbee was with Timothy on T.B.'s maiden voyage in their local park's paddling pool.

'I need to lower that sail a little,' murmured Granbee, and in a moment it was done! What a handy grandpa!

It was on Good Friday that Timothy ventured to the park to sail T.B. single-handed. An admiring group of children gathered round the paddling pool. Alongside, a river flowed invitingly. A voice encouraged Timothy to sail his boat in its more testing current. 'Let's see her really go!'

Timothy wound in the string and carried T.B. across the path. He pointed her downstream and let out the string. T.B. picked up speed and her sails billowed. She had been wonderfully made and drew gasps of approval from the bank of the river.

'Let her sail really free,' said that voice again. 'Let go of the string.'

Timothy half-heartedly countered the rumbles of agreement. 'No, I promised Granbee.'

'He'll never know,' said another, 'and we'll catch her at the bridge down there.'

Indeed, that would be safe enough, and everyone would see the full effect of Granbee's handiwork. Timothy let go.

T.B. was certainly a splendid sight, sails stretching as the wind swept her on towards the boy poised to gather her in as she approached the bridge.

'Let her go on!' exclaimed the voice, and the waiting boy on the bridge hesitated. In that moment T.B. sped on under the bridge.

It was only then that Timothy remembered the small, sharp waterfall lower down the river and already in sight. He couldn't keep up with his boat now as he pounded along the bank.

The group of admirers melted away to avoid any blame for the certain disaster. Although it was a shallow waterfall, the river was in full flow and it would be too great a hurdle for a little boat.

When Timothy reached the waterfall, he saw the full extent of the wreck. The sail had been torn by jagged stones, the hull had sunk beneath the foaming water and the mast floated on like a frail twig.

Alone and forlorn, Timothy stood on the bank. Only the string, now free from the boat, was within reach. Miserably he wound it round his paw.

He dawdled homeward across the grass, fighting back his tears. He was angry most of all with himself. What a bad Friday it was turning out to be.

The voice that penetrated his gloom was the one he least wanted to hear.

'Cheer up! It may never happen,' said Granbee.

'It just has,' muttered the crestfallen grandcub.

Grandpa took in the scene in a moment: the string, the river, the waterfall. Timothy's tears started to flow.

'Come now,' said Granbee. 'One waterfall's enough. Good job I've put my Wellingtons on.'

Through his tears, Timothy saw his grandpa wade into the frothing water to lift out the hull of the wrecked boat. Granbee returned to Timothy and those steely blue eyes were on him. Timothy almost wanted the telling-off that must be coming.

'I was thinking,' said Granbee quietly, 'if I hollow out this hull, I could put in an engine and make you a motor boat! I might have it ready for Sunday.'

Timothy's mouth gaped open in surprise.

'But,' continued Granbee, 'it will still need the string for you to hold on to.'

Grandpa, of course, was as good as his word and two days later presented Timothy with a shining motor boat. Its name was written in black on the side: 'The New T.B.' It was Grandpa's Easter Sunday present to Timothy, and even better than the biggest Easter egg in any sweet shop.

Helping children get to grips with the story

★ What is Timothy's grandpa like?
★ What reasons were there for Timothy to let go of the string?
★ Why did Timothy end up on his own?
★ What was Grandpa's big surprise?

Ways for children to express the story

★ Make a model boat out of bits and pieces, or from paper, using the instructions at the back of this book.

★ Draw a picture of the boat just coming to the waterfall or anywhere else on its journey.

Helping children to own the story

★ Timothy gave in to the voices of other children. Is it easy to do as we've been told when others are telling us otherwise?
★ What orders are we given? Is it always easy to keep them?
★ Grandpa gave Timothy a new start. What new starts does God give us on Easter Sunday?

Ways for children to live out the story

★ How do we know what are the right things to do? Is it always easy to do them?
★ Why did Timothy expect to be told off by Grandpa? When do we deserve to be told off?
★ Why should we be thankful that God gives us new starts?

Summer term

A story for Pentecost

Timothy Bear has a quiet time

✔ PSHE link

Skills, knowledge and understanding 1d: Pupils should be taught to think about themselves, learn from their experiences and recognize what they are good at.

✔ Bible link

On the day of Pentecost all the Lord's followers were together in one place. Suddenly there was a noise from heaven like the sound of a mighty wind! It filled the house where they were meeting. Then they saw what looked like fiery tongues moving in all directions, and a tongue came and settled on each person there.
ACTS 2:1–3

Since Easter, Timothy had been learning about listening, both at school and at church. At school, they'd found out how ears work, about ear trumpets and hearing aids, about animal ears and about listening to sounds going on around them.

'Often we're too noisy ourselves to listen out for things,'

said Miss Read. Her class understood what she meant.

At church, it was about how we can listen to God, and how we can understand what God wants us to do and be. 'It will soon be Pentecost. That's when God's Holy Spirit was heard and seen,' pointed out Reverend Moody. 'Let us tune in to God's Holy Spirit this year.'

Timothy finds listening quite hard. 'You're a fidget,' says Mrs Bear. Indeed, he's always one of the first out in 'Sleeping lions'. 'Sit still,' said Mr Bear the other weekend. 'I'll have to glue you down to that chair of yours if you don't.'

The next Saturday, Timothy decided to do something about it. He decided to try to be still... and quiet. He turned off the television and went to sit on the front doorstep with a book. He ignored his bicycle and his football.

It was such a change to be sitting so quietly. He heard the distant hum of traffic and then the bird song in the garden across the road. Then, closer to hand, he heard an urgent miaowing. Could it be a cat in trouble?

He followed the sound, and there behind a shrub, next door's kitten had its paw caught in the wire netting between the gardens. The more the kitten struggled, the tighter the paw was trapped.

Using his own paws skilfully, Timothy widened the hole round the kitten's paw and the released creature went indoors to find a saucer of milk.

Timothy resumed his quiet place on the doorstep. A woman was coming along the pavement, wearing a green woolly hat.

'Good,' said Timothy to himself, 'here comes Grandma.'

When the woman came nearer, so that Timothy saw the

face below the hat, it might have been Grandma's hat but it wasn't Grandma's head! Timothy had already said 'Hello.'

The woman said, 'What a kind bear you are. That's the first voice I've heard today.'

Thinking she might have been Grandma caused Grandma to be at the front of Timothy's mind. He couldn't get away from thinking about her. He went to find Mrs Bear.

'May I go to visit Grandma?' he wanted to know. Grandma lived very near to Timothy and he could get to her house without crossing any roads.

'What a good job you've mentioned Grandma,' said Mrs Bear. 'I've got some eggs for her and I've forgotten to take them to her. You can take them at the same time.'

It was turning out to be quite a morning. As Timothy was going in at Grandma's gate, he noticed something black under the hedge. It was a purse, quite heavy with money. Grandma would know what to do about it, so Timothy carried it carefully, with the eggs, up to the front door.

Grandma came to the door and took in with a glance the sight of her grandcub and his offerings.

'Wonderful Timothy!' she burst out. 'You've found my purse! I've looked everywhere for it and was just about to phone the police. Let's find you a drink and some biscuits.'

Timothy told his side of the morning's story.

'It was all because I decided to sit still and quiet,' Timothy began. When he'd finished, it was Grandma's turn to talk.

'Every morning,' she said, 'I try, too, to have a quiet time. This morning God was telling me how much he cares for me, especially now I'm on my own. And now you've come to help me. You're my Godsend.'

As he ate another chocolate biscuit, Timothy modestly supposed that he really was Grandma's Godsend!

Helping children get to grips with the story

★ Tell the children the story of the first Pentecost in the life of the church. The story can be found in Acts 2:1–12.
★ What were the reasons that led up to Timothy visiting his grandma that Saturday morning?
★ Why did Grandma say that Timothy was her Godsend?

Ways for children to express the story

★ Make a list of noisy things to do and then a list of quiet things to do.
★ Draw a careful picture of someone like Timothy's grandma who might come to your mind.
★ Make a collection of things that make loud sounds and soft sounds.

Helping children to own the story

★ Pentecost is about the coming of God's Holy Spirit—the Spirit of Jesus—into the world. In the story, what do you think happened because of God's Holy Spirit?
★ What good thoughts about kind actions come into your mind?

Ways for children to live out the story

★ Some time today, try to spend five minutes quite still and quite quiet. Listen carefully with your ears and see what thoughts come into your mind.
★ In what different ways might God speak to us through his Holy Spirit?

A story for Trinity

The clock party

✅ PSHE link

Skills, knowledge and understanding 4b: Pupils should be taught to listen to other people, and play and work cooperatively.

✅ Bible link

The Holy Spirit will come and help you, because the Father will send the Spirit to take my place. The Spirit will teach you everything and will remind you of what I said while I was with you.

JOHN 14:26

Timothy was next door with Mrs Centurion. He tries to pop in to see her at least once a week.

'Anything we can do for you?' asked Timothy generously.

'Well,' hesitated Mrs Centurion, 'there's my clock. It has suddenly stopped and I miss it so much.'

'Dad will put it right,' said Timothy.

Timothy has great faith in his dad's ability to put things right. Mr Bear has indeed mended many broken toys. He sees to the car. He put up the swing in their garden and built the rockery behind it.

'It's Saturday,' pointed out Timothy, 'so if I take the clock now, Dad should have time to put it right.'

'All right. If it's no trouble,' said Mrs Centurion.

Mr Bear smiled when Timothy presented him with the broken clock. He didn't go in for clock repairs, but he would have a look anyway. He opened up the back, and father and cub gasped at the array of wheels, springs and cogs that made up the workings of a clock.

A tiny screw had fallen to the bottom of the clock. Mr Bear knew that his paws were much too large and clumsy to deal with such a small screw.

'Timothy, I can't do it,' said Mr Bear. 'You might be able to do it with your smaller paws. That screw has got to go in there!'

Timothy could pick up the small-sized screw with his small-sized paws. Timothy could slot it into the hole. Timothy could begin to turn the screw to secure it. Mr Bear had found his specially small set of screwdrivers, so Timothy could tighten the screw into place.

'Give the clock a little shake,' advised Mr Bear. Timothy did and the clock started ticking again. It really did.

'Well done, mate,' said Mr Bear to the beaming Timothy.

Mrs Bear had seen what was going on.

'How about inviting Mrs Centurion round for a clock party this afternoon? I can make a special clock cake for tea, and I'm sure we can provide some entertainment.'

Mrs Centurion accepted the invitation eagerly and came round for the party at the agreed time. To begin with, they played a version of 'What's the time, Mr Wolf?' and then, as the weather was fine, they had a round of clock golf in the garden.

After that, it was time for tea. Mrs Bear's clock cake was greatly admired. The hands and numbers were made out of marzipan.

Next, Teresa played her part. She knew off by heart the rhyme 'Hickory, dickory, dock! The mouse ran up the clock'. At school they were learning a song about grandfather's clock, and she sang it to great applause at the end. Then it was time for Mr Bear to present Mrs Centurion with her repaired clock.

'You mustn't think that I repaired it,' began Mr Bear. He went on to explain how Timothy had put it back together again, following a bit of fatherly advice. He went on to talk about Mrs Bear's idea for a party and her skills at cake making. Mr Bear was making quite a speech, especially when he thanked talented Teresa for the entertainment.

'Now it's my turn,' said Mrs Centurion. She thanked each member of the Bear family in turn. She held up her precious clock.

'I'll be in time to get to church tomorrow morning, now my clock's working again. It's Trinity Sunday, when we remember how God United works so well together. Today it has been Bear Family United. It must be Quadnity Saturday!'

'I don't quite understand,' said Timothy.

'I'll explain it to you later,' promised Mr Bear.

Helping children get to grips with the story

★ How did Mrs Centurion's clock get repaired?
★ How did each member of the Bear family help to put on the clock party?

Ways for children to express the story

★ Draw a picture of what Mrs Centurion's clock might have looked like.
★ See how many nursery rhymes you know by heart.
★ What do you think Mrs Centurion said in her speech when she thanked each member of the Bear family?

Helping children to own the story

★ Can you think of things you can do that grown-ups can't do?
★ Do you know any words that begin with 'quad'? Can you work out what Mrs Centurion meant by Quadnity Saturday?

Ways for children to live out the story

★ What did Mrs Centurion mean by remembering God United on Trinity Sunday? What words do you know beginning with 'tri'? Do they help you understand 'trinity'?
★ How could your whole family help someone? Who might that someone be?

A story for Ascension day

In touch

Skills, knowledge and understanding 3g: Pupils should be taught rules for, and ways of, keeping safe, including people who can help them to stay safe.

 Bible link

Jesus led his disciples out to Bethany, where he raised his hands and blessed them. As he was doing this, he left and was taken up to heaven.
LUKE 24:50–51

Mrs Bear's friend was going into hospital for an operation, and Mrs Bear was arranging to look after her two children for a few days. As the friend lived a hundred miles away, Mrs Bear was going to stay there until Friday.

'I'll take Teresa with me, but you mustn't miss school, Timothy. You'll be all right, won't you?'

'Of course,' said Timothy with more certainty than he felt. It would be so strange not to have Mrs Bear around. Timothy couldn't remember a single day when she hadn't been there. Mr Bear would look after him, of course, but he would still be at work. Mrs Centurion had promised to collect him from school.

Timothy felt quite odd saying 'goodbye' on Wednesday morning before he went to school.

'I'll see you on Friday,' said Mrs Bear softly. 'Keep putting your best paw forward.'

It was one of Mrs Bear's sayings, and Timothy knew it was her way of telling him that she wanted him to carry on just as if she was around. Mrs Bear was finding it quite hard to say 'goodbye' now the time had come for it.

'Here's your packed lunch,' continued Mrs Bear when she saw that Timothy was in danger of forgetting it. 'It's a good job your head is screwed on tightly, or you'd forget that!' It was another of Mrs Bear's sayings.

When it came to lunchtime, Timothy Bear looked at his lunchbox more carefully than usual. Mrs Bear was now a hundred miles away but she'd still made sure he had his food.

There was a piece of paper inside the box as well. It was a picture of a lady bear and her cub—surely Mrs Bear and Timothy. Across the top it said, 'Don't leave a mess—crumbs in tums—love Mum.'

Timothy smiled to himself and cleared up especially carefully.

That evening, it was much quieter than usual in the Bear household until Mr Bear's mobile phone showed an incoming text message.

'It's for you, Tim, from Mum.'

Timothy was excited. He didn't get many texts and Mrs Bear must be still thinking about him all those miles away.

On Thursday morning, Mrs Bear sent Timothy a postcard that the postman delivered, and that evening there was a phone call. Mrs Bear's voice was as clear as if she was in the next room.

'I'll see you tomorrow evening,' ended Mrs Bear.

'I can't wait,' answered Timothy.

Friday evening came and, as it turned out, Timothy found himself on his own indoors while Mr Bear collected Mrs Bear from the station. Timothy didn't mind. Mum would be home again so soon—and Teresa too.

It would be good to do something as a welcome back. Mr Bear and Timothy hadn't managed much housework in Mrs Bear's absence and Timothy guessed that the shelf in the lounge, with all their precious ornaments on it, would be dusty. He brought in the set of three steps from the kitchen. When he inspected, the shelf was indeed thick with dust!

Carefully, Timothy removed the ornaments one by one and dusted them and the shelf with the duster from under the stairs. It was when he had just replaced the final ornament in the furthest corner that he lost his balance and crashed to the carpet from the steps.

The only damage done was to his paw. It hurt. He couldn't put much weight on it and it was swelling up larger than the other three.

He remembered Mrs Bear's advice. 'Wrapped in something very cold makes a sprain right as rain!'

He knew where the frozen peas were kept in the freezer. He limped to the kitchen. He found the pack of frozen peas.

Timothy went back to the settee in the lounge and made himself as comfortable as he could, with the television on and his paw wrapped in the ice-cold bag of peas.

A few minutes later, Mr Bear arrived back home with Mrs Bear and Teresa. What a reunion! What excitement! Timothy Bear explained what had happened to his paw. After a fatherly talk about keeping safe, Mr Bear tidied up the steps and put them back where they belonged.

Mrs Bear admired the shelf and said she'd forgotten to dust it for a whole month.

'Now for something to eat,' said Mrs Bear. 'We'll have sausages, chips and peas.' She took the still-frozen bag from Timothy.

'I don't want any peas that have been round Timothy's paw,' giggled Teresa.

'That's all right,' smiled Mrs Bear. 'It's not any old paw; Timothy always puts his best paw forward!'

Helping children get to grips with the story

★ Tell the children the story of Jesus' ascension to heaven. The story can be found in Luke 24:50–53 and Acts 1:6–10a.
★ It was hard for Jesus' friends when he went away to heaven— much harder than for Timothy when Mrs Bear travelled to look after her friend's children. In what ways did Mrs Bear keep in touch?
★ What did Timothy decide to do as a 'welcome home' present? What happened? How might the accident have been prevented?

Ways for children to express the story

★ Draw what you think was on the paper inside Timothy's lunchbox.

★ What might have been the text message that Timothy received from Mrs Bear? Make up a reply from Timothy.

Helping children to own the story

★ Has someone very important to you ever had to go away? Talk about it.

★ What other good 'sayings' are there for us to live by?

★ What good things came out of Mrs Bear's going away?

Ways for children to live out the story

★ On earth, Jesus could only be in one place at one time. In what ways does he keep in touch with us from heaven?

★ What might Timothy have learnt because Mrs Bear went away?

A story for St George's day

Dragons

 PSHE link

Skills, knowledge and understanding 4a: Pupils should be taught to recognize how their behaviour affects other people.

 Bible link

Love each other as brothers and sisters and honour others more than you do yourself.
ROMANS 12:10

At first, Timothy Bear didn't realize he was up against dragons. Dragons were in story books!

His sister Teresa was getting on his nerves. Brother and sister usually got on well together, but Teresa was going through a particularly selfish time. She'd always been better at saving money than Timothy and so she had more money for sweets.

'You never share any of your sweets with me,' moaned Timothy.

Another thing was that Teresa always wanted to be first,

and because she was younger she usually got her way. She was the first to move in chess, the first to choose cakes, always clamouring to eat the first pancake.

And Teresa always told on him. Timothy was allowed to stay up 15 minutes after his sister had gone to bed. Even though she couldn't yet tell the time properly, Teresa's voice would come calling down the stairs. 'Isn't it Timothy's bedtime yet?'

Mr and Mrs Bear would be reminded and Timothy would have to go to bed.

On the eve of St George's day, Mrs Bear told Timothy the story of St George before he went to sleep. He heard how George, the knight in shining armour on a white horse, galloped to the rescue of a beautiful princess held prisoner by a wicked dragon.

Mrs Bear told the story of the fight in thrilling detail. Timothy's imagination was working overtime.

'There aren't too many dragons around these days,' pointed out Timothy.

'Perhaps they don't look like dragons now,' said Mrs Bear. 'Perhaps today's dragons are called "Telling lies", "Laziness" and "Being selfish".'

'I know someone who's been captured by the dragon "Being selfish",' murmured Timothy. Perhaps he should do something about it!

Timothy had a pleasant dream. He was dressed in armour, sitting on a white horse, and taking on a fierce, fiery dragon in front of a cheering crowd. When he released the princess, she turned out to be Teresa!

Next day, Timothy went into a wide-awake battle. When

his weekly comic was delivered, he offered, for a change, that Teresa should look first at the part of it she liked.

At playtime, for a change, Timothy found Teresa in the playground and spoke kindly to her and her friends. He even pointed out that Mary's shoelace was undone and did it up for her.

At home, after school, for a change, Timothy listened to Teresa reading her schoolbook and said how good she was.

Teresa wondered if Timothy would teach her some more chess. 'You go first, for a change,' she said with a smile. 'And you might like to share my bar of chocolate.'

When it came to Teresa's bedtime, she was so tired that she was asleep as soon as her head touched the pillow. Timothy made the most of his extra time downstairs.

'Well,' he said, 'I think I've seen off one or two of Teresa's dragons.' He told his parents the story of the day and his determination to rescue Teresa.

'Well done, Timothy,' said Mrs Bear.

Mr Bear joined in. 'Yes, well done, Saint Timothy! It sounds to me as if you sorted out some of your own dragons at the same time.'

Helping children get to grips with the story

★ Children could hear the story of St George and the dragon in greater detail.
★ Can you remember Mrs Bear's modern-day dragons?
★ How was Teresa being selfish?
★ What was the twist in the end of the story about Timothy?

Ways for children to express the story

★ Draw or paint pictures of St George and the dragon.
★ Make a list of ways you would like others to share with you.
★ Make a list of things you would find difficult to share with others.
★ Draw or make dragons, and write labels giving them each a name of a modern-day dragon.

Helping children to own the story

★ Can you add to Mrs Bear's list of modern-day dragons?
★ Can you remember times when you've been cross about having to go to bed? What happened?

Ways for children to live out the story

★ In what ways can you get rid of modern-day dragons? Remember, you may have been captured by one or two of them!

A story for early summer

The bluebell woods

 PSHE link

Skills, knowledge and understanding 2f: Pupils should be taught that they belong to various groups and communities, such as family and school.

 Bible link

Love your neighbours as much as you love yourself.
LUKE 10:27B

Mrs Bear seems to know when to arrange a visit to the bluebell woods. The bluebells are always at their most beautiful. It was so warm this year that Mrs Bear took her folding seat as well. She pointed out the area of the woods in her sight that Timothy could explore.

'I won't be able to tell you from the bluebells,' said Mrs Bear. Timothy was wearing his blue Bearchester United Cubs tracksuit. He had great fun. He crawled back carefully through the bluebells and came so close to Mrs Bear that she had no idea he was there. In fact, she started to call out for him to come for his snack, and he was only a couple of metres away. What fun! He made his mum jump a bit when he said, 'I'm just here!'

Timothy was more adventurous after his snack and went over towards the fence that Mrs Bear had pointed out as a boundary. He heard sounds of someone crying... sobbing. Timothy crawled through the bluebells to investigate.

In a shallow dip in front of the fence sat someone he recognized, crying her heart out. It was the tallest girl in his class at school. Her name was Barbara Pole, but as she was so tall she liked being called Beany.

It was just as well she couldn't see him. He'd hardly ever spoken to her before. Timothy turned to slither away.

'My ankle! My ankle!' sobbed Beany.

Timothy couldn't leave her like that, even though he didn't know her very well. She might not be found by anyone else before it got dark. Timothy stood up so that his head was above the bluebells.

Beany was so amazed, she stopped crying. She was grateful for any company—even a bear cub. She blurted out her story. She'd been running and twisted her ankle falling over a root of the tree. She was too heavy for her mum to carry, so Mum had had to go for help. Beany had found it frightening being on her own as well as coping with the pain in her foot.

'I'll stay with you now,' volunteered Timothy. 'I know a few jokes.'

'Great,' said Beany, recovering quickly.

'How do you count cows?' asked Timothy.

Beany shook her head.

'With a cowculator!' Timothy was pleased to see a pale smile cross Beany's face.

'Who swings through the vines?' asked Timothy.

Again Beany shook her head.

'Tarzan of the grapes,' answered Timothy.

'You're a poet and I didn't know it,' grinned Beany.

Minutes later, Mrs Pole arrived with her husband.

'You have kept calm,' said Mrs Pole, pleased that their daughter had been so sensible.

'Well, I did have some help,' said Beany, pointing towards her classmate. But Timothy had vanished, merging again into the bluebells, his mission accomplished.

When he got back, he found Mrs Bear fast asleep. Timothy coughed quietly to wake his sleeping mum.

'I must have dropped off for a moment or two,' said Mrs Bear. 'What have you been up to?'

'Oh, I've had a few expeditions. This and that. And I helped a bean pole in distress.'

'You do say the most amazing things at times,' smiled Mrs Bear.

Helping children get to grips with the story

★ Why was Timothy unsure at first about helping Beany?
★ In what ways did Timothy help Beany in the end?
★ What did Mrs Bear think of Timothy's adventures?
★ Tell the children the story of the good Samaritan. The story can be found in Luke 10:25–37. In what ways was Timothy like the Samaritan in the story?

Ways for children to express the story

★ Draw or paint a picture of Timothy among the bluebells.
★ In the story Timothy was camouflaged well. Can you think of any other examples of camouflage?
★ Tell some good jokes. If you are in a group, you might make a collection of them in a book.

Helping children to own the story

★ Remember times when you have been in pain or frightened. What helped you most?
★ Can you think of people you might not help immediately if you found them in trouble?

Ways for children to live out the story

★ Think of someone in your class or group that you don't know very well, and try to get to know them better.
★ Is there someone in trouble that you could help?

A story for Father's day

A welcome load of rubbish

 PSHE link

Skills, knowledge and understanding 2h: Pupils should be taught to contribute to the life of the class and the school.

 Bible link

God sees that justice is done, and he watches over everyone who is faithful to him. With wisdom you will learn what is right and honest and fair.

PROVERBS 2:8–9

When Timothy sends his Father's day card this year, it is going to contain an unusual message:

'Dear Dad. Thank you for being such a welcome load of rubbish!'

Here's what happened. Timothy was drinks monitor for the week. One of his duties was to take the crate of empty bottles and cartons every afternoon and put it neatly by the dustbins for the milkman to collect. Timothy did his task with care. He likes to help the smooth running of his school.

A boy in Timothy's class was much less keen to help. In fact, Paul preferred to hinder, and he seemed especially to dislike Timothy. As soon as Timothy returned from seeing to the crate, Paul put his hand up to ask if he could go for a drink. Miss Read agreed, as it was a hot day and, for once, Paul had enquired politely. But Paul did not go for a drink. Instead, he went outside the school kitchen and upset the crate that Timothy had left so carefully. What a mess! Mrs Bear happened to be going round to Grandma's and saw what happened over the hedge.

Mr Mason, the school caretaker, discovered the crate and complained about it to Miss Read. She had a sharp word with Timothy at the end of school.

'I'm really disappointed, Timothy,' she said. 'Make sure you do your job better tomorrow.'

Timothy was quiet when he arrived home. It was hard sorting things out, especially when he'd really tried to do his best. By bedtime Mrs Bear had the whole story out of him, and in her mind she remembered what she had seen.

'We'll make sure it doesn't happen tomorrow. It's just as well your dad will be collecting our brand new dustbin!'

Timothy did not understand what she meant, but as he felt comforted he found it easy to get to sleep.

If you had been watching the school dustbin area the next afternoon, you would have seen Mr Bear adding a brand new dustbin to the number there. Then you would have seen him climbing into it and sliding the lid over the top, leaving a gap above so that he could breathe.

He could also see out of the bin. He saw his cub, Timothy, come round and carefully leave the crate so tidily, only two or three metres from where he was hidden.

Moments later, Mr Bear saw Paul approaching, looking over his shoulder to make sure he was not being watched. Paul crouched down to begin to upset the crate.

'That's very nasty, young man!' boomed a voice from inside the dustbin.

Paul froze in his tracks. He looked round to see who it was. No one there. He must be hearing things. He crouched down again.

'No, Paul,' said the same voice. 'Leave it alone.'

Paul had had enough. It was almost as if the dustbin was speaking! Paul turned on his heel and, for once, was glad to get back to class. Mr Bear climbed out of his dustbin and resumed his journey home, carrying the dustbin and smiling to himself.

Mr Mason was smiling too. He had seen the episode by the dustbins from the kitchen window. Before the end of school, Mr Mason was helping with the clearing up in Miss Read's class.

'Miss Read,' asked Mr Mason, 'could Paul take this black sack of rubbish to the dustbins, please?'

'No! No! I won't,' shouted Paul.

'That's very rude,' pointed out Miss Read. 'Whatever's the matter?'

'We've got talking dustbins,' blurted out Paul.

'Oh dear,' said Miss Read. 'Perhaps you need to explain why you think that is!'

Before Timothy went home, Mr Mason had a chat with him to let him know what he had seen, and to say sorry about his mistake the day before.

So now you know why Timothy wrote what he did in his Father's day card!

Helping children get to grips with the story

★ In what ways does Timothy help the running of his school in the story? In what ways does Paul hinder the running of his school?

★ Why did Timothy write what he did in his Father's day card?

★ Why did Paul refuse to get rid of the black sack of rubbish?

Ways for children to express the story

★ Make a Father's day card.

★ Draw a picture of Mr Bear peeping out from the dustbin.

★ Make a pop-up model with someone popping up out of a dustbin.

Helping children to own the story

★ Complete the sentence: 'Paul deserved to be frightened because…' or 'Paul did not deserve to be so frightened because…'

★ Has a grown-up ever helped you out of an unfair situation?

Ways for children to live out the story

★ Timothy had to cope with being blamed for doing something that wasn't his fault. Has that happened to you? Talk about it.

★ Make a list of things you might write in a card to someone who is looking after you as well as Mr Bear was looking after Timothy.

A story for the time of the school play

The good prop

 PSHE link

Skills, knowledge and understanding 1d: Pupils should be taught to think about themselves, learn from their experiences and recognize what they are good at.

 Bible link

If you are cheerful, you feel good.
PROVERBS 17:22A

Timothy's school is famous for its school plays. They do two a year—one that includes a nativity scene at Christmas and a second one in the summer. This summer it was to be 'Charlie and the Chocolate Factory'.

Timothy wasn't given an acting part this year. 'You can look after the props, Timothy,' said Miss Read. 'You make sure that everything is in the right place on the stage.'

Everyone was looking forward to the time when the play would be ready to perform in front of parents and other friends. They practised hard. The children with the main parts had lines to learn; the children who would be the Oompa-Loompas in Mr Wonka's factory were the best singers and had songs to learn.

The chocolate-making machine looked very real, but in actual fact it was a wide board with the machine painted on the front and a hinged supporting post holding it up from behind. Timothy put chalk marks on the stage floor so that it was in just the right place for the Oompa-Loompas to sing from behind it.

Miss Read was pleased with her choir. 'But if only they would look as if they were enjoying it,' she was heard to remark in the staff room.

The great day arrived and everything was ready. The actors were being dressed and were just about containing their excitement.

Timothy was checking the props. The chocolate machine had slipped from its usual position. Timothy went to put it right.

To his horror, he saw that the post was no longer fixed to the back of the board. The screws had worked loose from the hinge and fallen to the floor. He stood the machine up on its own but there was no way it would stay upright without its support throughout the performance—and that performance was just moments away from beginning. There was not even time to involve Miss Read.

Timothy could hear the audience becoming quiet on the other side of the curtain. Timothy decided what he would do. He would stand behind the machine and hold it upright with his back. After all, he had been put in charge of props. He would be completely hidden from the audience.

Moments later, the play began. It was even better than it had been in rehearsal. Everyone remembered what to do and what to say.

Charlie Bucket and Grandpa Joe held it all together with Mr Wonka. Augustus Gloop was the first child to disappear, and then the Oompa-Loompas gathered behind the machine to sing a song. What a surprise when they saw a smiling Timothy Bear holding up the chocolate machine! They smiled back as they sang their song.

As the other characters disappeared one by one in the story, the singing got even better and even more joyful. By the time it was Mike Teavee's turn to vanish, Timothy was pulling faces and conducting with his paws. Miss Read hadn't believed her choir could sing as well as it did at that performance.

The mothers, fathers and friends said afterwards what a marvellous performance it was. 'Better than ever,' they said. They had enjoyed every minute.

'I wonder how Miss Read arranged for those Oompa-Loompas to sing so well and smile so much at the same time. That was the best part of all,' said one member of the audience.

Even Miss Read didn't find out how until afterwards, but you knew about it all the time. Didn't you?

Helping children get to grips with the story

★ Why did Timothy get the part he did in the school play?
★ What was the extra part that Timothy needed to do when the play was actually performed?
★ What brought the best out of the Oompa-Loompas?

Ways for children to express the story

★ Draw your own picture of a chocolate-making machine. You might even make a model.
★ Draw a picture of Timothy propping up a board with his back.

Helping children to own the story

★ Talk about a play that you have been part of or seen as a member of the audience.
★ Was Timothy's part in the play important?
★ Did it matter that Timothy was never seen by the audience in the whole play?

Ways for children to live out the story

★ Talk with each other about being a good member of a group or a team. Talk about being a 'star' or a 'back-room' person.
★ What has to be done to put on a play, besides actually acting in it?

A story for summer

The beach day

 PSHE link

Skills, knowledge and understanding 2e: Pupils should be taught to realize that people and other living things have needs, and that they have responsibilities to meet them.

 Bible link

Be humble and consider others more important than yourselves.
PHILIPPIANS 2:3B

Timothy Bear loves the seaside, and best of all he enjoys a beach day with his family. On one particularly sunny day, they set off early, piled up with buckets and spades, a large picnic hamper and all the things that Mrs Bear could possibly think they might need.

'Let's settle here,' said Dad, pointing to a spot on the beach that was level with the steps. The tide was right out, so there was plenty of space on the sands.

When they were organized, Mr Bear had an idea.

'We'll build a sandcastle,' he said to Timothy, 'a castle that's the biggest on the beach.'

Mr Bear's like that, and soon the sand was piling up and the castle taking shape. It would have a spiral track round the outside, so that a ball could travel down into its moat. Just as Mr Bear was digging out the moat, Timothy spotted a donkey that had come to give rides.

'No,' said Dad, 'not until we've finished the castle.' He had guessed that Timothy would want a ride.

As soon as the castle was completed, Timothy was allowed to go for his donkey ride, but by now the queue stretched as far as the ice cream man.

Timothy took his place at the back and waved to Mum and Dad to let them know he was all right. He stretched up on tip-paw to see the front, and saw the donkey taking each child in turn along to the pier and back.

The donkey passed mothers and fathers who were reading, grandparents who were nodding asleep and babies dribbling on to the sand.

Patiently, Timothy waited for his turn to come. At last he was third from the front. He was hot and getting a little hungry. Then there was a commotion up by the steps. A woman was trying hard to push a girl in a wheelchair through the sand.

'I'm sorry, Sophie,' she said as they came closer to Timothy. 'You can't have a donkey ride. Look at that queue! We'd never get back in time for dinner.'

Sophie, who for some reason could not walk, looked sad but said nothing. Then Timothy did one of the best things he'd ever done.

'Excuse me,' he said shyly, 'Sophie's welcome to take my place.'

Sophie's face lit up and so did her mother's as Timothy gave up his place.

It was a long walk to the back of the queue. It went as far as the Punch and Judy tent by now. When he reached the end, Timothy could just glimpse Sophie being lifted on to the donkey's back to enjoy her ride. She passed the mothers and fathers who were reading, the grandparents who were nodding asleep and the babies dribbling on to the sand.

It had been a long walk back for Timothy, and it was an even longer wait for his turn. The sun was high in the sky and it really must have been dinner time, but in the end his turn came. Timothy handed the man the money.

'Oh no,' the man smiled. 'I saw what you did for that little girl. Your ride will be free.'

The man lifted him up for his ride on the donkey. Timothy waved to Mum and Dad as he set off towards the pier.

'What a brilliant beach day,' thought Timothy as he passed the mothers and fathers still reading, the grandparents still sleeping and the babies still dribbling on to the sand.

Helping children get to grips with the story

★ Why was there a long queue for donkey rides even before Timothy started to queue?
★ Why did Timothy have to wait much longer for his turn in the end?
★ Why was Timothy enjoying his beach day so much at the end of the story?

Ways for children to express the story

★ Make a list of all the things Mrs Bear might think her family needs for a beach day.

★ Make a beach picture. You might include mothers, fathers, grandparents and babies!

Helping children to own the story

★ What are your favourite things to do on the beach?

★ Do you think that what Timothy did was 'one of the best things he'd ever done'?

★ Talk about an animal ride you might have had.

Ways for children to live out the story

★ What sand models would you like to build?

★ Timothy gave up his place in the queue. Do you think he did the right thing? Can you think of times when you would like to give up your place or give up your turn?

Index of PSHE links

Knowledge, skills and understanding

1b   A Good Friday story...76

1d   A story for Christmas..44
      A story for Pentecost 88
      A story for the time of the school play 113

1e   An Advent story 40

2b   A story for Epiphany 54

2c   A story for Guy Fawkes day...31
      A story for Easter Sunday..81

2e   A story for harvest 18
      A Palm Sunday story 72
      A story for summer 117

2f   A story for early summer 105

2h   A story for Father's day 109

3a   A story for Lent 64

3g   A story for Ascension day..96

4a   A story for Hallowe'en..27
      A story for St George's day 101

4b   A Shrove Tuesday story 60
       A story for Trinity 92

4d: An autumn day story...23
       A story for Mothering Sunday...68

Breadth of study

5b   A story for the new school year 14

5e   A story for Remembrance..36

5h   A snowy day story 50

Index of Bible links

Old Testament Bible links

Psalm 145:9	A Shrove Tuesday story	60
Psalm 147:15–16	A snowy day story	50
Proverbs 2:7	A story for the new school year	14
Proverbs 2:8	A story for Guy Fawkes day	31
Proverbs 2:8–9	A story for Father's day	109
Proverbs 3:27	A story for Remembrance	36
Proverbs 4:18	A story for Hallowe'en	27
Proverbs 11:25	A story for harvest	18
Proverbs 17:22a	A story for the time of the school play	113
Proverbs 19:8	An autumn day story	23

New Testament Bible links

Matthew 2:1–2 and 7–10	A story for Epiphany	54
Matthew 2:11	A story for Christmas	44
Matthew 4:4	A story for Lent	64
Matthew 21:1–2	A Palm Sunday story	72
Luke 2:7	An Advent story	40
Luke 10:27b	A story for early summer	105
Luke 24:50–51	A story for ascension day	96
John 13:34	A story for Mothering Sunday	68
John 14:26	A story for Trinity	92
John 19:16–18	A Good Friday story	76
John 20:1	A story for Easter Sunday	81
Acts 2:1–3	A story for Pentecost	88
Romans 12:10	A story for St George's day	101
Philippians 2:3b	A story for summer	117

Instructions for making a paper boat

1. Take a sheet of A4 paper and fold in half widthways (Figure 1).
2. Find the centre point along the folded edge of the paper and fold the corners down to meet in the middle, forming a triangle (Figure 2).
3. Open out the remaining edge of the paper and fold each side back towards the triangle, forming a hat shape (Figure 3).
4. Holding the lower edge (the 'brim' of the hat) at the centre point on both sides, open the shape out and refold it to make a diamond. Tuck the loose ends neatly under each other on both sides (Figure 4).
5. Lay the diamond shape flat and fold back the open end to match the triangle shape at the top of the diamond (Figure 5).
6. Turn the paper over and repeat with the other side (Figure 6).
7. Once again, holding the lower edge at the centre point, open the shape out and refold it to make a diamond shape (Figure 7).
8. Take hold of the outer points on both sides of the top of the diamond and gently pull them apart in an outward direction (Figure 8). This will form the boat shape, with the small centre triangle acting as a sail.
9. Gently shape the paper around the base of the sail so that the bottom of the hull is slightly flattened, allowing the boat to stand (Figure 9). The finished boat will be strong enough to float on water for a short length of time.

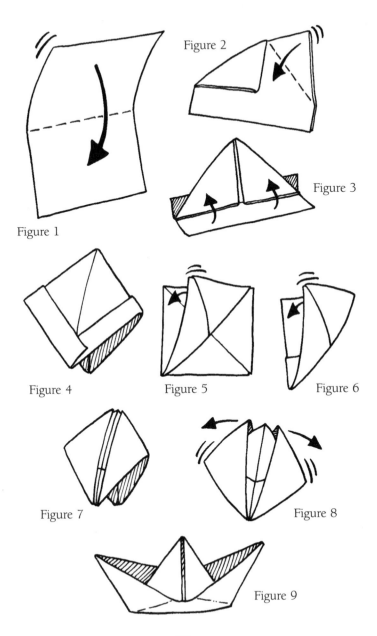

Figure 1

Figure 2

Figure 3

Figure 4

Figure 5

Figure 6

Figure 7

Figure 8

Figure 9

125

barnabas

Resourcing **Storytelling, Drama, RE, PSHE/Citizenship, Circle Time, Collective Worship** and **Assembly**
in primary schools

- Barnabas Live creative arts days
- INSET
- Books and resources
- www.barnabasinschools.org.uk

visit our website at **www.barnabasinschools.org.uk**

Barnabas is an imprint of brf   *BRF is a Registered Charity*